Wild Bill Donoho: From Corrupt Cop to Raceway Mogul

By

Shena Newberry Wilder

Deep Read Press

www.deepreadpress.com

615-670-1725

LAFAYETTE, TENNESSEE

deepreadpress@gmail.com

First Deep Read Press Edition.

Published in the United States of America

ISBN (Paperback): 978-1-954989-29-0

ISBN (Hardback): 978-1-954989-30-6

Published by:

DEEP READ PRESS

Lafayette, Tennessee

www.deepreadpress.com

deepreadpress@gmail.com

Acknowledgments

I want to thank many who helped me write this book, especially my dear husband and loving children. I desire this book to inspire my children and grandchildren to research our rich history and draw inspiration, creativity, and pride in their lives. I also want to thank my Lord and Savior for the numerous blessings He bestows on me daily.

Dedication

I dedicate this book to my brother, Anthony Lee Newberry, who left this world too soon, and my sweet grandma, Lillie Mildred *Donoho* Whitley.

Contents

"It is remarkable how closely the history of the apple tree is connected with that of man."

– Henry David Thoreau

Prologue

What motivates a man of meager beginnings? Money and power, of course. How would a young man in his early twenties manifest a life of great power and wealth? The answer is simple: networking. Networking in the day of William "Bill" Donoho did not include the internet or computers of this day and time. Networking in his day meant one friend knew another friend and introduced each to their friends. While living at his home, Jennings Creek in Jackson County, Tennessee, time was spent "thinking, pondering, and reflecting" upon his immediate circumstances and how to change the situation. While working in the fields plowing, planting, and harvesting crops necessary for sustaining the lifeblood of a large family, I suspect my Great-Uncle Bill used his time, along with the necessity of invention, to plan and design opportunities to find work, to make his life different, and to ease the pain of hunger in his belly.

Introduction

In this book, I hope to convey my great-uncle's life story of being born into poverty and moving to Nashville, Tennessee, to fulfill his dream of getting rich. When first arriving in Nashville, he worked as a barber, building up a successful business; however, cutting hair was not his preferred occupation – it merely paid the bills. Barbering did prove to be profitable as it helped him network with people, creating an infinite number of relationships. That would later prove the old wise adage that sowing seeds inevitably brings about an abundant harvest from an orchard rooted deep within the ground of the hearts and minds of people from all over the nation.

Upon a chance meeting, a client with whom he had developed a friendship gave him a good reference for obtaining a job as a policeman with the Davidson County Police Department. The excitement of the good guy versus the bad guy intoxicated my Great-Uncle Bill. Some months later, the United States entered World War II. Bill Donoho was drafted into the Navy. At the end of World War II, he returned to his life in Nashville. Over time, exhilarated with power, he thrived in his position and traveled up the ranks of the Police Department, becoming one of the most influential administrators of the disciplinary office of Nashville. His reputation created fear in the hearts of law violators in Nashville. Corruption within the lifestyle was substituted for healthy character and morals.

Several years later, my great-uncle's power and authority engulfed him. He began to believe in his infallibility. He seemed to think he was Elliot Ness, one of the 'untouchables.' When he was actually charged with extortion and making prostitutes and gambling houses pay for police protection, my great-uncle was flabbergasted. Ultimately, he was arrested and convicted in federal court for tax evasion, much like Al Capone, the mobster and leader of organized crime in Chicago. The Federal prosecutors had their work cut out for them as his first trial was determined to be a mistrial. During the second trial, my Great-Uncle Bill Donoho was finally convicted and sentenced to serve time in Federal Prison out of state.

He appealed to the United States Supreme Court, but they refused to hear the case. He returned to his home in Nashville and began vigorously promoting the Fairgrounds Speedway. My great-uncle had acquired the land for the Speedways and, along with partners Bennie Goodman and Mark Parrish, invested in stock-car racing in the mid-1950s. The Fairgrounds Speedway was a financial windfall lining Bill Donoho's pockets with a plethora of cash and bringing significant tourism to Tennessee. My great-uncle fell from grace only to rise from the ashes and give back to Nashvillians and the great state of Tennessee, or did he?

Part I of this book will transport you back to the early 1900s. One example is the automobile, which had been improved upon due to the assembly line and manufacturing production in the industry, providing jobs to many. Other innovative people were showing the progression of technology and ideology. It had only been four decades since the Civil War in the United States. The U.S. was not interested in involvement in other world affairs, yet World War I managed to pull the United States inside its grasp. The women's suffrage movement was at the height of giving women greater freedoms. Jim Crow Laws, especially in the South, were also being implemented to limit people of color from having equality. The Emancipation Proclamation opened the doors for people of color to be freed from slavery, and to be actively recognized as part of the 'human' race. Tragically, it would be years before absolute equality between the races became the norm.

Part II of this book will share how communication via the telephone, invented by Alexander Graham Bell, was well entrenched in modern society by the time young Bill came of age to explore life on his terms. In Bill's early 20s, he moved to Nashville, Tennessee, to make his mark on the world. He would gain employment as a police officer with the Metro Nashville Police Department. This author will uncover the behavior of a small-town farm boy who moves to the big city of Nashville to create his 'Field of Dreams,' and answer the questions about the actions that impacted Bill Donoho as a person with an indelible need for power and money. This author will share Bill Donoho as a man of high society, a leader, yet a man who truly believed he was above the law, both a prisoner of his narcissistic mind and a prisoner in a federal prison convicted by the federal government. And convicted daily in public opinion through the newspaper's detailed descriptions of his life, crimes, and association with people whose lives drastically differed from his own.

Part III of this book will share Bill's motivation in developing the Nashville Speedway and how it impacted Nashville, Tennessee, and the global racing community. This author will strive to explain the many lives affected by his greed and his 'need for speed.' Information will be shared about friendships and partnerships that liquified due to the fluidity of greed that frothed out of every pore of his body. However, my great-uncle was a brilliant man and a magnificent negotiator, who had a genuine connection with everyone he met. The last years of his life will explore the legacy he left behind, impacting those of Nashville and the world.

Notably, the asphalt racetrack first hosted NASCAR racing when it opened in 1958, under the ownership and leadership of William "Bill" Donoho Sr., Mark Parrish, and Bennie Goodman, and it became one of the most popular speedways on the circuit.

My Great-Uncle Bill's determination, ambition, and energy were drilled daily into his son. William James Donoho Jr., affectionately known as Jim, followed the pattern of his father. In his early years, he exhibited initiative and cleverness. He was accomplished in several areas of his life, including having an extraordinary musical talent. In high school, he was a tennis star. By his college years, he was a mogul like his father in business. Jim also experienced many failures. His personal life suffered because of two public and expensive divorces. Financially, he had to file for bankruptcy. However, like his father, Jim persevered through every setback by holding his head high and rising up with new revelations and ingenuities to be successful.

Overall, this book will strive to expose the internal conflicts and psychological motives that drove my great-uncle to hunger for more and more wealth and personal, as well as public, power, regardless of any action or evidence to prove differently. Lastly, this author will share personal expression and thoughts about William "Wild Bill" Donoho, who was a public felon whose greed worked to perfect the city of Nashville and the state of Tennessee. Through the brilliance of the promotion and development of tourism, my great-uncle contributed to Nashville and the people of Tennessee in many ways other than what lined his pockets. Karma can have a way of using negatives to turn positives into possibilities.

1. Wild Bill's Beginnings

"All badness is spoiled by goodness. A bad apple is a good apple that became rotten. Because evil has no capital of its own, it is a parasite that feeds on goodness."

– Fulton J. Sheen

William James Donoho
"Bill"

During the early 1900s, the same mountains that gave Jackson County, Tennessee, its beauty also made travel difficult in the days before paved roads and steel bridges. Both the Cumberland and Roaring Rivers extended across the county. Timber and farming were the primary occupations in the county since its establishment, and riverboats of bygone days passed through the county daily, carrying passengers, merchandise, agricultural produce, and lumber products.

The community of Jennings Creek sat on the western side of Jackson County, bordering the eastern side of Macon County. Jennings Creek is named after the creek, which meanders through the portion in the west of Jackson County, Tennessee, and settles near the community of Whitleyville, Tennessee.

My great-grandparents built a small cabin on Jennings Creek. Up until just a few years ago, the large rock fireplace chimney stood tall in the sky. Eroded and weathered, it ultimately collapsed back onto the rich soil surrounding it. Modern progression of colonizers and the advancement of societal needs took up land for agricultural endeavors and domiciles where the home stood, and succumbing to erosion was often accompanied by progress.

The recently invented automobile would occasionally cross through the fields and pastures. Still, it would be another decade or more before the people of Jennings Creek (the wealthy) would travel the area in the new motorized vehicles. In 1915, rural Americans walked or rode a horse everywhere, lived in three-generation homes they rarely owned, ate almost as much lard as chicken, and spent Friday nights dancing to player pianos or sing-a-longs. In short: Life was not much more accessible in this era than for the early pioneers, especially in rural America.

Nashville, Tennessee – the seat of Tennessee – was just like other cities in the South. Order must be instilled so the town could progress into the new age. It was 1937 when young William "Bill" Donoho traveled to Nashville to work as a barber.

William "Bill" James Donoho was born in 1915 to Radford and Rene Donoho, the fifth of 10 children right after the beginning of World War I. Radford was a farmer by trade, and Rene was a housewife. Their family lived on little. Garden food, tobacco, and strawberries were grown for selling. Wild game provided protein for the family. Radford, Rene, and the children were thin and impoverished. Yet, pride overtook any prospect to ask for charity.

Young William "Bill" Donoho was intrigued by the automobile. He eagerly explored the design and engineering of cars. Fascinated by their speed, he occasionally raced with drivers from the saddle of his horse. However, the Donoho family saw very few automobiles, as their primary means of transportation were walking by foot or riding by horse.

The automobile gave people more personal freedom and access to jobs and services. It led to better roads and transportation. Industries and new jobs were developed to supply the demand for automobile parts and fuel. The car gave women more freedom to see the world than they had ever had before. More freedom meant more independence. Electricity had not yet appeared in rural areas, but about half the urban homes had it by 1925. Communication via the telephone was well entrenched in modern society by the time young Bill came of age to explore life on his terms. In young adulthood, he was hired as a police officer for the Davidson County Police Department soon after moving from rural Jackson County to Nashville in the late 1930s. However, as a teenager who had not had the chance to experience much more than church and farm life, William "Bill" Donoho was fascinated with all the new technology, especially engines and speed.

****

This author seeks to share knowledge of a man born into this world with a hungry belly. William "Bill" Donoho and the other children in this family were always hungry, living hand-to-mouth. Being born a boy meant he was a commodity to his father, and he would become a worker in the farm fields like his older brother Cap Wesley as soon as he was of age. The days were long. Winters were cold, and summers were scorching hot. With so many mouths to feed, learning to live with hunger was their way of life. Young Bill Donoho decided to force his way upward, out of poverty and into a society that respected and honored his dedication to greatness, leaving behind the squalor of destitution.

Bill finished school with an eighth-grade education. He labored in the tobacco fields, corn fields, and log woods to help his father support the family. However, when an opportunity for mischief came along, Bill was ready to jump aboard. Bill was 15 when he and his friend were walking down the road in the community of Willette, Tennessee. Wint Johnson drove down the street and asked the boys if they would like a ride. The boys eagerly and excitedly jumped in his truck. Wint stopped the truck in front of Bedford Newberry's house when they were to part ways. He went to speak with Mr. Newberry. When Mr. Johnson returned to the truck, he became angry as he realized several of his cigarettes were missing.

Experiences of the utmost excitement prompted the 15-year-old Bill to be stirred to the core with interest in the automobile, which would only grow stronger as he matured. As far as the cigarettes were concerned, both boys protested their innocence as they ran away from Wint Johnson's fury.

Shortly after, Bill moved to Nashville and found work at a barbershop cutting hair and shaving men and boys of all ages. At 24, he became a police officer for Davidson County Police Department in Nashville, Tennessee. Just when he was getting his bearings together and learning all the requirements of his position in the police department, he was drafted into the Navy in October 1942, after the attack on Pearl Harbor.

World War II was raging in the Pacific. President Franklin Roosevelt had been reluctant to enter the war until the Pearl Harbor Naval Base was attacked in Hawaii on December 7, 1941. William "Bill" Donoho left his position with the Davidson County Police Department and his young bride Jesse Mildred, to serve his country. Mildred kept herself busy as a cashier while her husband fulfilled his obligation to the war effort. She was an avid gardener, enjoyed cooking, and passed the time with her beloved pets. After the war in 1945, and after being Honorably Discharged, Bill returned to his bride and his life with Davidson County Police Department. However, his position as an officer had been taken; he was appointed as a Radio Dispatcher for the department.

Over the years, Bill dedicated his life to building his career in law enforcement and dabbling in racing motorcycles and stock cars. In 1948, Bill and Mildred welcomed their first child, a son named honorably after his father, William James Donoho Jr., also known as Jim. Moving up the ranks in the department also allowed Bill and Mildred to move upward within Nashville Society. They participated in trap shoots and were honored with trophies and recognition for their achievements and accuracy. The *Tennessean* often posted pictures of Bill and Mildred showing off their shooting skills. Bill joined the American Legion and reigned supreme with Mildred, enjoying all the comforts of diplomacy and reputation with their rise in social status.

****

The United States had watched with unease as circumstances led up to The Great War. War of a different kind was happening in the lives of rural Tennessee as families worked hard just to stay alive. It was a battle to survive. The small farm owned and tirelessly worked by Radford and Rene Donoho welcomed the birth of a daughter, Viola, who died in 1910 on November 24, making the early years of their marriage very sad. Cap Wesley was born the following year. He survived and lived to be 91 years old. In 1914 Rene and Radford were surprised by the birth and death of twins Sammie D. and Effie Lee on July 17. Unfortunately, they were both too small and did not survive the difficult birth. Sadness loomed over the Jennings Creek Valley until December 8, 1915, when William "Bill" James Donoho arrived, fighting for life and limb. William James whimpered softly and weakly as he gasped for air with his tiny lungs. Uncertain of the tiny boy's ability to grow and thrive, Rene did all she could to nurse him and keep him warm during the cold winter of 1915-1916. Rene prayed and felt blessed as each day passed with little William "Bill" surviving. His little body worked each day only to fight for the next. By spring 1916, Radford and Rene felt confident that their little Bill's determination to live was secure. Bill was a fighter, never giving in, never giving up. This strength and determination would drive him in later years, pushing him to the edge of uncertainty, only to arise triumphant from every snare that dared to hold him back from his destiny.

On March 11, 1918, Rene and Radford welcomed a daughter named Lillie Mildred. Like her brother before her, Lillie Mildred was determined to live. She endured great hardships as a girl child of the era. She persevered until her death in June 1993.

Lillie Mildred was my grandmother. As a child, I practically lived at my grandparent's home. I helped with gardening, picking strawberries, and canning apple jelly from the orchard on their farm. In the winters, during hog killing, I helped render the lard used for cooking and baking. Eating fresh cracklings and pork skins was a treat when everything was finished. My grandmother taught me to sew, quilt, and cook. Everything about being with her made me feel loved and safe.

Rene and Radford welcomed four more children over the next few years after Lillie Mildred; thus, a large family with hungry faces met at the table each morning before dawn and each evening when the workday was over. As stated earlier, Bill was a fighter, and he fought for life, food, and recognition as the stronger brother.

2. Cop/In the Navy

"Relationships are like apples: they can be sweet and satisfying. But once you bite into a bad one, it's hard to go back to the barrel again."

– John Avery

Young patrolmen were often teased because of their eagerness to make their mark on the force. One such incident occurred on October 29, 1941. What started as a simple public drunkenness arrest ended with Patrolman W.J. "Bill" Donoho driving a banana-loaded peddler's wagon through heckling crowds. At the same time, his distressed partner, Patrolman W. D. Monohan, lamented about all the embarrassment. "Why do these things always happen to us?" Demeaned, he took the ribbing with a good measure of humility. At Eighth Avenue South, the patrol officer had found Efron Hoover, 54, from Rutherford County, driving a fruit wagon while impaired. Duty said they should take him to the Police Station. However, it didn't tell them how to take the wagon to the station. It was up to Donoho and Monohan to figure it out. Monohan put Efron Hoover in the squad car and eyed Donoho speculatively. With resignation in his voice and a large sigh, Officer Donoho climbed upon the banana wagon, losing some as he made his way to get aboard. He quietly drove the wagon through the streets of Nashville.

Incidents such as this had occurred often, embarrassing the young patrolmen in their eagerness to protect the streets of Nashville and impress their commanders. Both young officers had figured out early on that keeping the streets safe by doing their duty regularly created fodder for citizens and other officers because of the predicaments and dilemmas they often encountered.

When the United States entered World War II, there was a rallying cry to support U.S. troops. Rationing items such as sugar, rubber, gasoline, meat, coffee, butter, and canned goods were sacrificed to help with the war effort. Rationing worked on a coupon system so that quantities and allotments were equalized. Americans were asked to do their duty by doing without. President Roosevelt's Executive Order 8875 created the Office of Price Administration (OPA) to place a ceiling on prices and limit consumption by rationing. A violation of rationing regulations was considered a serious crime.

In his eagerness to impress, City Policeman Bill Donoho set an investigation into the violation of federal tire rationing regulation in motion. Officer Donoho arrested Marcus Hackerman and seven others and charged them with conspiracy to violate the federal tire rationing regulation. Federal Warrants Charged – Purchases made without Certificate. This is believed to be the first in the United States "Under the Second War Powers Act" and "the regulations issued thereunder the buyer of rationed or restricted commodities are equally guilty of violations of the laws as the seller." Rubber had been restricted in an effort to preserve resources for the needs of World War II.

"These so-called 'black markets' cannot exist unless there is someone to create an illegal demand." William J "Bill" Donoho was credited with opening the forefront of a nationwide crackdown by the Office of Price Administration against purchasers of new tires who did not have rationing certificates. Jack Bondurant, the local representative of the United States Office of War Information, said that as far as he knew, the federal charges of purchasing new tires without the proper certificates from the War Price and Rationing Board were the first ever made in the United States. The seven defendants and the charges against them were listed in the federal warrants. Perry Dale of the Dale Brokerage Company was arrested for purchasing four new tires and six new tubes. Marcus Hackerman, a convicted numbers operator, and Gary Henderson conspired to transfer by the sale of the new tires without the proper certificate. Henderson was also accused of selling 30 new tires and 32 new tubes. Henderson was in the Davidson County Jail on state charges of robbery, growing out of the alleged theft of the tires he was accused of selling illegally. Henderson allegedly stole the tires and tubes several weeks earlier from the George Cole Motor Company, where he was employed. Credit went to Officer Donoho and the 26 members of the Nashville Police Department for setting in motion the investigation that broke up the alleged black market of new automobile tires and tubes. Donoho, who had been on the police force for two years, used his initiative to investigate those who violated the law while on duty and off duty.

Donoho reported to his superior, Sgt. Milliron; Donoho and Patrolman Jack Murphy began an investigation that led to the swearing out of the warrants for the alleged law violators. Deputy U.S. Marshals Sam Burton and Hugh Biffle were accompanied by Police Officer Donoho when the warrants were served. The men later pled guilty, were fined, and sent to the county workhouse. As stated earlier, making his name known in Nashville and throughout Tennessee helped grow the William "Wild Bill" Donoho name and empire.

Twenty-four-year-old William "Bill" Donoho was drafted into the Navy to serve his country. While awaiting his orders to report to the War Office, young William "Bill" Donoho continued proving his value to the Nashville Police Department.

On October 11, 1942, William "Bill" James Donoho, city motorcycle officer and youngest man on the city police force, was sworn into the U. S. Navy. He was sent to the Great Lake's Naval Training Base in Chicago, Illinois, for six weeks of basic training immediately after the ceremony. He left his wife, the former Jessie Mildred Smith of Red Boiling Springs, Tennessee, to serve his country.

William J. Donoho Sp(G)3c Instructor in primary gunnery at the Naval Air Technical Training Center at Memphis and former motorcycle officer on the Nashville police force, was awarded the expert rifleman and expert pistol shot medals by Captain James C. Monfort, the commanding officer of the center. To qualify for the pistol medal, Donoho had to score close to 240. He scored 236. The expert rifleman medal was awarded to persons making 175 out of a possible 200 at distances of 100 and 200 yards; Donoho rolled up 189. The marksman had been an instructor in primary gunnery for 18 months. In addition to this class, he also instructed a class of officers in pistol, rifle, and machine gun.

On November 5, 1945, Bill Donoho left the Navy with an Honorable Discharge. Afterward, he enlisted with the National Guard and the American Legion, serving accordingly for the next several years. The American Legion is an organization that provides life-changing help to former military personnel, their families, and communities in thousands of ways worldwide. Help consists of financial help, cash grants, donated goods, disaster relief, labor, networking, volunteerism, and advocate assistance with personal issues. "Wild Bill" Donoho was a proud member of the American Legion for all the positive attributes, but it also offered young Bill something more: connections with other veterans, some of whom had great power and influence within Nashville.

He was excited to return to his home and his beautiful wife. Yet, due to a financial deficit within the Davidson County Police Department, he could not return to his previous job. He was, however, hired at a lower rank. During Donoho's time in the Navy, the Nashville City Police Department's finances had been mismanaged. Officers often had to pay out of their pockets for sparkplugs for patrol cars. Three patrol cars had to be sold for junk to pay utility bills. Several department members took up a collection to buy a few balls of string to tie identification tags on recovered stolen property. Operating expenses, payroll, and repairs to patrol cars were in grave danger. Operating on the current budget for the current fiscal year, there was a $1,500 shortfall for meeting payroll for the last two weeks of August.

City officials were very concerned that if the present wave of petty crime, common to most cities, continued to rise in Nashville, a police department with rundown equipment would have difficulty stopping it. The town depended on individual officers' pride and the spirit of the men to keep things going. Police officers worked overtime without the necessary equipment and financial compensation for the additional hours that were needed to keep Nashville safe. The morale of the department was low and needed immediate enlightenment.

The department's complement of rolling stock — most of it so worn that it couldn't move more than once or twice a week — included: nine cars in the radio patrol division, two homicide cars, and ten in the detective division. It was a regular event for squad car officers seeking to apprehend criminals or answering a call to have their vehicles break down. If it was a call to be answered, officers often made the rest of the trip by bus. If it was a fleeing criminal, the criminal's flight was successful. The police department could buy only two new Fords to supplement its supply of worn-out automobiles, even though in the previous months, the city council appropriated $20,000 for new rolling stock for the department. Commissioner Mays made every effort to get additional new cars from dealers. The city hall faction didn't support him in his attempt to bring enough pressure to ensure the delivery of a more significant number of new cars.

Out of sheer necessity, Commissioner Mays was forced to dip into the new car fund for money to pay for major repairs for present motor equipment due to the continued fear of operating a police department without patrol cars. Using these funds prevented the need for repair at the city garage. During the present period of street repairs, the department faced the heaviest demand in its history for officers to direct traffic. Traffic would stall daily during rush hours without officers at all uptown corners and many corners in the outlying districts. In the face of this demand, the critical factor could easily mean lost lives.

The Nashville Davidson County Police Department was like other departments, like the fire department, crossing our fingers and hoping nothing would happen. The average policeman, who works a regular shift of eight hours a day, six days a week, and spends an extra four hours a day from four to five days a week appearing in court, does not feel that his $180 a month salary is an overpayment during the present times, especially since he must buy and maintain uniforms, pistols, and all other equipment he wears. The city's financial plight prohibited law enforcement from adequately performing their duties.

Being an honorably discharged veteran of the United States Navy should warrant some exception within the administration of Davidson County. Serving and dying for our country should be treated with great respect and honor, not punishment, due to mismanagement of funds within a city of this size. It was a personal offense to Officer Donoho to accept a demotion in light of recent occurrences within our country.

3. Great Shooting Skills

"You have to be burning with an idea, or a problem, or a wrong that you want to right. If you're not passionate enough from the start, you'll never stick it out."

– Steve Jobs

Donoho's passion for public recognition for his shooting skills continued making his name known within the ranks of Nashville Society. On August 18, 1946, he swept the floors clean as he competed in the weekly shoot at the Nashville Gun Club. The Radio Patrolman scored 50 / 50 in winning the trapshooting event. He then won the skeet laurels in a shoot-off with H. G. Payne and C. J. Cochran. First place in the skeet division was decided in a shoot-off when Donoho, Payne, and Cochran each posted scores of 47 / 50. In a different firing, Donoho won with a 24 / 25 score. Cochran and Payne each posted 22 / 25 in the shoot-off.

Perfecting a skill is only helpful if dedication and determination are targeted in a person's heart. In September 1947, Bill Donoho, a Nashville motorcycle police officer, won the bi-state pistol championship match at the annual convention of "the Mississippi-Tennessee Peace Officers Association in Biloxi, Mississippi." Donoho shot a 48 and 49 out of a possible 50. He and Lt. John B. Milliron of Nashville were also members of a five-person Tennessee team winning their match. Other members were William Raney of Memphis, and Carl Black and Herman Whalen of Knoxville. Milliron was

28

named Director of the association. The Mississippi Commissioner of Public Safety elected President Sgt. N. L. Luther, of the Nashville Homicide Staff, as the Vice President.

Bill Donoho's experience with a pistol dated only to the day he joined the police force and his wife's only to 1943. Still, they were talking of a trophy room. The *Nashville Tennessean Magazine* published an article titled "Shooting for Skill," in which Bill Donoho and his wife Mildred demonstrated their shooting skills as a sport. Bill Woolsey wrote an article about the couple and their extraordinary lives.

4. Finding Corruption

"As time goes on, we get closer to that American Dream of there being a pie cut up and shared. Usually, greed and selfishness prevent that and there is always one bad apple in every barrel."
— Rick Danko

How does the lousy apple show up in the barrel? This question can be answered by the simple explanation of educating oneself in the culture of how criminals make money from enterprises rubbing against the underbelly of society.

In October 1947, the *Tennessean* reported that several Nashville businessmen, including several public officials, were scheduled to be called before the Davidson County grand jury to testify concerning gambling activities of an alleged local bookie joint. Their names appeared on payoff sheets seized by City Patrolmen Morgan Smith and Bill Donoho in a raid on a place off Fourth Avenue North, Nashville. The payoff sheets showed businessmen and some public officials had placed bets on horse races. Their names were turned over to Tom Aldred, special Grand Jury Officer with the District Attorney General's office. District Attorney General J. Carlton Loser said Officers Smith and Donoho would be allowed to examine and present the payoff sheets and other evidence seized in the raid. In contrast, only four persons were indicted by the Grand Jury.

Attorney General Loser stated that he had not conferred with the officers concerning the evidence and had not seen the list of wagerers but had only told Smith that he would be allowed to present the case to the Grand Jury. State warrants charging Hugh H. Wilson and Charles R. McHaffey with gaming law violations were sworn out by Officers Smith and Donoho. Only minutes before, City Court Judge Andrew Doyle dismissed charges of owning and operating a gambling establishment against the two men on the grounds of an illegal search.

The patrolmen pursued charges of encouraging, promoting, or assisting in betting on horse races against the two men and keeping a place for inspiring, advertising, or helping in making bets on horse races. However, through a general session court clerk's error, three warrants were issued against McHaffey and only one warrant against Wilson.

Signing the warrants was General Sessions Court Judge John Draper. Wilson posted a $250 bond and McHaffey posted a $500 bond to guarantee their appearance in General Session Court to face the charges. In an ironic twist, at the same time, the patrolmen signed a similar state warrant against Joseph Castleman of the Classification Center in charges growing out of two raids on an establishment named Matt's Place, which had been dismissed in Criminal Court. Castleman posted a $500 criminal court appearance bond, thus waiving the preliminary hearing to send the case directly to the Grand Jury. Patrolmen Smith and Donoho had first arrested Castleman for owning and operating a gambling house. Still, these were dismissed by Judge Doyle on the grounds of the illegal search. Officer Morgan Smith and Patrolman Donoho left city court immediately after the charges had been dropped. They raided Matt's Place again and arrested Castleman for keeping a disorderly house. Eleven persons were also detained during the afternoon raid for loitering about a gambling house. Still, they forfeited short cash bonds by not appearing in city courts, as did the other people arrested. During the last afternoon raid on Matt's Place, the officers intercepted a telephone call that led to the bust.

The two men arrested on charges of loitering about a gambling house in connection with the arrest of Wilson and McHaffey also forfeited small cash bonds when they failed to appear in city court. The charges were dismissed against Wilson and McHaffey after Judge Doyle denied Officer Smith's request to amend the warrants against the two by adding the charges to the state's warrant. Wilson and McHaffey, with their attorney Wiley Wilson Jr., accompanied Officers Smith and Donoho to the courthouse where the state warrants were sworn out. Castleman voluntarily came to the clerk's office later and posted bond. Officer Smith asked Castleman to remain in the city courtroom after the charges had been dropped. Still, Judge Doyle told the man to "go ahead unless Officer Smith has a new warrant against you now." After a moment's hesitation, Castleman left the courtroom.

Learning the game of knocking the apple off of one shoulder only to have its target shot off of another is seen in the actions of the mismanagement of Courtroom drama. In the end, the men in question were only mildly inconvenienced since the judge dismissed each case and refused the requests by Officer Smith to amend the warrants. Perhaps the clerical and/or judicial errors resulted by accident. However, a proud United States Veteran trying to build a career in law enforcement and his police comrades felt extremely frustrated that their efforts to fight crime went awry with the justice system not utilizing evidence against apparent "law violators."

5. Locating Vice

"Business executives need to start by spelling out and communicating their values. Then they need to lead by example. This means getting rid of the bad apples and declining opportunities that bring instant wealth at the cost of selling one's soul."

— Vivek Wadhwa

Will Mosley, a 42-year-old Black man, was released on a $500 bond within 10 minutes after his arrest on charges of violating the state lottery law. After receiving information that the man was breaking the law, Mr. Mosley was arrested by off-duty Motorcycle Officers Morgan Smith and Bill Donoho. Following the arrest, Commissioner Seth Mays said that Officers Smith and Donoho 'did their duty' in arresting Mosley, and added, "It is the sworn duty of every member of the police department to make arrests when they know the law is being violated."

Commissioner Mays had previously issued orders that no police officer was to depart from his assigned territory while on duty. Officers Smith and Donoho had arrested men off their territory and were praised because they were not on duty. Commissioner Mays did not see a conflict between his previous orders and Officers Smith and Donoho's actions regarding Mosley. The officers said they confiscated approximately 2,500 tickets from Mosley's 1947 Sedan. The tickets showed bets ranging as high as $2.

A pattern of how the underbelly of Nashville worked and how law violators skirted around the legal ramifications of their actions emerged. Opportunities for networking with people from both sides of the law became evident. Nashville officers learned how to moonlight as "uniformed law violators." Only officers who lived by a moral compass and had loyalty to their oath as protectors of the general welfare of the people would resist the chance to supplement their meager pay. Many Peace Officers of Nashville came to know exactly how to use each side of the law as an opportunity to put more money in their pockets. Throughout Nashville's history, these men who had been children of the Great Depression era understood the security of filling one's wallet as an added necessity for preserving and improving their security.

Under questioning, Mosley gave his occupation as a 'meat cutter.' Mosley denied he had a boss in the numbers racket, stating instead that he was "fooling around." Smith and Donoho said they arrested him on orders of Chief John Griffin. Chief Griffin praised the officers for making the arrest and added, "The city charter makes it mandatory that an officer of the law make an arrest when he sees the law being violated. They have my permission to enforce the laws of the land." Mays instructed all officers to turn in to Chief Griffin the names of persons they knew violating gambling or liquor laws. However, the higher-ranking law officers did not quickly clarify conflicting information on responsibilities regarding when and where law violators could be arrested.

Toward the end of October 1947, Patrolmen Morgan Smith and Donoho raided a basement establishment late at night. They arrested the operator and four other men. The alleged violator was released on a $50 bond of a charge of owning and operating a gambling establishment. The officers confiscated ten decks of playing cards and a 'hi-lo' dice device. Booked on a charge of loitering about a gambling establishment was John "Tuck" Hurn, whose disappearance in a cave near Chattanooga and subsequent reappearance in New York City was slated as a publicity stunt. His shenanigans had incited nationwide publicity several months prior. Also arrested were Herold Greer, William Perry, and Tom White. These four were released under a $10 cash bond.

The two traffic patrolmen who had worked as a team in raiding alleged bookie establishments and other illegally operated places were split up in November 1947. There was great speculation as to why the duo was split up. This caused fodder for other officers conjecturing that those in higher positions or city government wanted to reign in Officers Donoho and Smith. Traffic Inspector Willard Jett said the changes were merely routine in personnel assignments. Patrolmen Smith and Donoho had been conducting vice-raids in various city sections, sometimes making the arrests off duty. The Davidson County Grand Jury indicted several persons arrested by Officers Smith and Donoho on tippling, violating liquor storage regulations, and violating state lottery laws.

It might be interesting to note that my Great-Uncle Bill Donoho and Officer Morgan Smith had the opportunity to examine the list of individuals identified as gambling and violating the law before presenting it to the Grand Jury. Were the 'influential' individuals on the list trying to break up the information gleaned by the officers? In future chapters, we will examine the processes of getting rich quick by illegal means and who benefited from the raids. Were the officers justified in arresting law violators, or were they playing the game to learn how to make their fortunes? Apples rot much faster when thrown in the bag with other apples. Is it possible that individuals involved in illegal wagers were moving the officers around Nashville like chess pieces, utilizing each of them for interests that benefited the law violators on both sides of the law?

Was someone, or even a group of individuals, trying to avenge the raids and officers investigating information from informants? In early November 1946, two break-ins and thefts were reported to the police. Motorcycle Patrolman Bill Donoho, the owner of a Shell gasoline station, was broken into and approximately $50 in cash was taken. Ironically, NASCAR was developed by individuals who owned gasoline service stations. This author will explain more about that later in this book. Donoho was mechanically-minded and had been fascinated with the automobile since his youth. Investing in a service station was definitely an obvious choice for "Wild Bill" Donoho.

Mrs. C. H. Payne said someone took her purse while shopping and $93 was taken. The Consolidated Products Company was ravaged by somebody through a locked door. The perpetrator entered through the side door, and a radio valued at $15 was stolen. Police theorized that the petty theft and crimes that plagued William "Wild Bill" Donoho were possibly by individuals or factions who were avenging their arrests. Other theories included the possibility that he was keeping his name in the newspapers, growing his recognition and power within the city of Nashville.

6. The American Legion

"I pledge allegiance to the Flag of the United States of America, and to the Republic for which it stands, one Nation under God, indivisible, with liberty and justice for all."

In early July 1950, the American Legion Post No. 5 named five men to office. Lieutenant Leslie Jett, the 28-year-old of the State Safety Education Division, was the youngest man ever elected as commander of Nashville American Legion; W. J. Donoho, a sergeant of the City Police Force, was chosen Vice-Chief, with H. E. Ball appointed Adjutant. Complete election returns were announced at the War Memorial Building after a day of balloting. Twenty-three men were elected to new positions in the American Legion. Immediately following the announcement, Commander Jett announced plans to re-equip and re-outfit the band of Post No. 5 before the state convention in August, and the National Convention in Los Angeles scheduled for next October. Jett stated that the accomplishment of the band program, which includes new uniforms and instruments and other plans for the upcoming conventions, were the first items to be considered after assuming his Post. Everyone who wanted to be 'someone' affiliated themselves with the American Legion. This organization provided a perfect place for networking between members. A large portion of cream rose to the top, just as soft clouds rise within the sky. However, the wind blew wildly as time passed, and the clouds, along with the cream crop of Nashville, began swirling unchecked by the justice system.

In 1952, William N. Tune was jailed on disorderly and offensive conduct after he allegedly parked his car in what police said was a no-parking area and refused to move it. Sgt. William "Bill" Donoho explained that there was no parking on the curb. This angered the patron so much that he challenged the officer by not complying with the order. Sgt. Donoho called his superiors and a wrecker. Mr. Tune was arrested, and his car was hauled away. When Mr. Tune started to walk away, he was quoted as yelling at the officer. "I'll pay $10,000 before I pay that unjust $2 parking ticket." William "Bill" Donoho continued to make enemies as he patrolled up and down the streets of Nashville, exerting his authority over every supposed law violator.

****

A squirrel-shooting hill boy, firing through shimmering heat waves and gusty winds, won the Tennessee National Guard's state rifle title. The champion was 22-year-old Herman Taylor Jr. of McMinnville, a rifle section squad leader in the guard's company G, 173rd Armored Cavalry Regiment. Taylor's 227 points out of a possible 250 on a course fired at 200, 300, and 500 yards with the M-1 Garand Rifle topped the efforts of the best guard marksman from units throughout Tennessee. Among those he outshot were marksmen who previously held national honors, one of those being 1st Lt. William "Bill" Donoho. Others who made the rifle team had scores ranging from 188 to 165. "If the boys knew what went on up here today, I think all of them would be shooting at squirrels, rabbits, and tin cans like I've been doing," Taylor said. This year, Major General Sam T. Wallace, the State Adjutant General, restored the Volunteer State to national marksmanship competition for the first time since 1939. Ten years had passed since Donoho had been drafted into World War II, learning his skills as an expert shooter. He was complimentary of Private Taylor's shooting abilities. Being from rural Jackson County, Donoho had eaten many squirrels and other wild game in his youth. He easily related to the young man from McMinnville, Tennessee.

7. Liquor and More Vice

"I wish to live to 150 years old, but the day I die, I wish it to be with a cigarette in one hand and a glass of whiskey in the other."
— Ava Gardner

In July 1952, Donoho could have quenched his parched mouth as he worked his assigned territory. Two automobiles, loaded with 80 cases of bonded whiskey worth $5,000, were forced to the curb on Hermitage Avenue by police who arrested drivers of the cars for illegally transporting liquor. When whiskey is "bonded," the spirit has been made, aged, and bottled according to a specific set of guidelines. The Bottled in Bond Act of 1897 was created to provide consumers with a guarantee of quality when it comes to their whiskey.

The drivers halted their cars without a chase. One of the men was armed. The whiskey was confiscated. The two men were both residents of Clinton, Tennessee. One was also charged with carrying a weapon and was freed on a $1,500 signed bond. The other was released on a $1,000 bond. City court hearings were held where City Police Sgt. Bill Donoho and Patrolman Bill Dunaway said they received a tip that two "cats" were being loaded with liquor at St. Charles Liquor Store at Fourth Avenue North. The officers said they rushed to the scene as the cars pulled away from the curb. The suspected lawbreakers were followed to Hermitage Avenue near Wharf Avenue. Donoho turned on his police siren and waved the two vehicles to the curb. "What have you got in your car?" Donoho asked. The men stated smugly that what was in their car belonged to them. The men agreed to allow their vehicles to be searched. The officers noticed that the cars were equipped with extra-duty springs necessary for hauling heavy loads. Officers stated that the back seats in both vehicles were missing. Whiskey was found packed under the floorboards covered with blankets. Somebody packed the trunks of the cars with the bonded whiskey.

Donoho said the two men got out of their cars with their hands lifted in the air. Both "cats" were searched. When they arrived at police headquarters, the man in the second car told officers that he was taking the liquor to Anderson County and had been paid $36 for the trip. The man said he had never made a run like this. Pleading, he said that his wife was pregnant, and he needed the money as he'd been out of work. He said he and his friend did not load the liquor in the cars. "We came to Nashville, parked the cars, and then went to a movie. After the movie, we returned to the loaded cars." Donoho said they were traveling leisurely; unaware police were tailing them. The man in the first car refused to make a statement on the advice of his attorney. However, he did admit he had made the same trip from Anderson County and back with whiskey on previous occasions. The officers said the two men denied they brought whiskey into Davidson County. Anderson County is a dry county, according to police. Neither of the two men had previous police records in Davidson County. The liquor was confiscated and placed in the office of Police Chief Ed Burgess.

The sequestration of whiskey prompted the police department to announce to operators of mixing bars and businesses that sold liquor that the doors would be padlocked if evidence was found that the establishments were selling illegal whiskey. The District Attorney General promised this after the successful raids of four places by Sgt. Donoho and Patrolman Bill Dunaway, whereas four operators were arrested. The officers stated they made whiskey buys in all the establishments before having warrants sworn out against the operators. All four owners posted $50 cash bonds. Meanwhile, the officers raided a tavern that catered to African Americans, arresting 14 customers on loitering charges and the operator for conducting a disorderly house. Donoho said the raid broke up dice and card games. Police Commissioner John Milliron had assigned the two officers indefinitely to a Vice Squad to clean up taverns and mixing bars where illegal whiskey sales were being made. He said military police and beer distributors lodged complaints of illicit liquor sales at several enterprises.

The recent public display of police intervention prompted Police Commissioner John B. Milliron to organize a permanent city police Vice Squad headed by Police Sgt. Bill Donoho. The squad was ordered to raid beer joints, honky-tonks, and mixing bars throughout the city without partiality or discrimination. The newly formed Vice Squad felt great pride in having higher-ups endorse the incursions. Milliron said he had discussed the issues of lawbreakers with Sgt. Donoho, and that it was his duty to use all available resources to sanitize Nashville. The commissioner insisted that the raids chosen would be at random.

The police and fire commissioner also denied any political significance to the appointment of the squad. He said the only motive was to mop up the city of dirt and grime. The appointment of Donoho came as a surprise in some quarters, in as much as it had been reported the sergeant was 'exiled' to East Nashville, along with Sgt. Morgan Smith, because the two officers continued making raid visits to Printer's Alley, the uptown center of nightlife and mixing bars. Milliron said there was no truth in these reports. He said Donoho and Smith were switched to East Nashville to improve the presence of the police system. By restricting Donoho and Smith to East Nashville, police calls from that section were cut in half. "They were two active sergeants, and the fact that complaints were reduced in East Nashville proves they did a good job."

Bill Donoho's authority was enhanced due to twelve persons charged with tippling, who were fined a total of $600 in city court by Judge Andrew J. Doyle. The tippling cases represented the work of Sgt. Donoho and Patrolman Bill Dunaway, working under direct orders from the Police Commissioner in quelling the illegal whiskey sales in Nashville. So practical was Donoho's and Dunaway's work that the Commissioner appointed additional officers to serve under Donoho in the clean-up. These officers made a continual effort to keep the city clean. Each violator was fined $50, which in 1952 was considered a significant sum of money.

A 47-year-old North Nashville man was arrested by members of the city Vice Squad and charged with violating the state lottery law. His name was Wade Tolliver, a Black man, from Nashville. Sgt. Donoho stated Mr. Tolliver was arrested in a shoe-shine parlor which he operated on Charlotte Avenue, and Vice confiscated 24,000 tickets, six pay-off tapes, and $559 taken in payoffs that were found in Tolliver's possession.

Bill Donoho's popularity within society continued, and in 1953, he was awarded a National Guard Commendation. The citation accompanying the ribbon praised Donoho's service from December 1949 to the end of the previous year in teaching pistol marksmanship within the National Guard. Another Nashville policeman recently named by Major General Wallace for meritorious service was Inspector Richard W. Jett, who served active duty as a Lieutenant Colonel with the Army. Later, 11 High Officers of Tennessee's Military Department were awarded commendations for the National Guard Distinguished Service Ribbon for outstanding service in their posts. The awards were signed by Governor Gordon Browning, Commander-in-chief of the state's military forces.

8. NASCAR Promoter

"Auto racing, bullfighting, and mountain climbing are the only real sports... all the others are games."

— *Ernest Hemingway*

A group of Nashville sportsmen leased the stock car racetrack located at the east end of the Jefferson Street bridge. The track – a quarter-mile oval called the Legion Bowl – owned by the Amusement Facilities, Inc., was leased by the newly formed group called the Nashville Speedway, Inc. for six years. As spokesman for the group, Bennie Goodman, Race Director, said, "There will be an entirely new policy at the new Nashville Speedway this year. The track is in the process of being rebuilt and is to be chemically treated, making it dust-free. Completely new facilities are being added to make the races an enjoyable evening's entertainment. There will be no alcoholic beverages sold on the premises. We desire to make the new Nashville Speedway the best racing oval in the South. New safety features have been added. A much speedier track is in store for some 100 drivers in the Nashville area." The opening date was set for early Spring. Officers of the new group included Bill Donoho, President; Bennie Goodman, Vice President; and Mark Parrish, Secretary-Treasurer.

Spurring Bill Donoho toward adrenaline highs, such as confiscating whiskey from whiskey runners, included vacationing in Georgia and North Carolina, the birthplace of

NASCAR. Junior Johnson, the first winner of NASCAR, began his career in racing as a bootlegger who realized that the engine must be able to outrun the authorities of Appalachia. Donoho relished the opportunity to become a political powerhouse beyond the reach of legitimate legalities. He used networking entities of liquor, loitering, prostitution, and gambling houses to further his agenda.

Bill Donoho endured the appearance of a public relations setback in April 1953. Police Chief Ed Burgess wiped out the department's Vice Squad because it "had failed to curb gambling" throughout the city. In issuing his order, the chief declared: "A gambler can operate only if the police department allows him to." Henceforth, the enforcement of gambling and vice laws would rest with the best patrolmen under the supervision of the three department inspectors: Inspector Boner, Inspector Hosse, and Inspector Muller.

The officers of Vice Squad members were returned to regular duties as patrolmen. Sgt. Donoho was one of two policemen reprimanded earlier in the year for using city workhouse prisoners to work at their homes.

In a statement directly to *The Nashville Tennessean*, Sgt. Donoho defended the operations of the Vice Squad. "Our record is open and speaks for itself. Despite the ridicule we received from the rest of the department, the Vice Squad members are proud of their service record. We have made more gambling cases and closed more places in the short time we have been on this duty than the entire police department combined. In eight months, we closed 22 places and made almost 1,900 cases. Our record is clean, and the Vice Squad cleared vast amounts of debris from our city." With Donoho's new endeavors of Stock Car Racing at the Fairgrounds Speedway, his time and influences focused elsewhere with "his need for speed." He had found a new opportunity to feed his adrenaline junkie addiction.

9. On the Take

"In the Second Amendment, it's not about hunting, it's not about target shooting, it's about protecting your home and your family and your life."

— Ted Cruz

Nashvillians respected Sgt. Donoho's skills as a marksman, and an incident exhibiting his talents was demonstrated when a young Henry Nichols discovered the depths of Sgt. William "Bill" Donoho's shooting skills. Sgt. Donoho halted Nichols, with two well-placed bullets in the tires of Nichols's car after a wild 20-minute car chase. Donoho said when he drove up behind Nichols at Eighth Avenue North and Jefferson Street, he "dropped his car in low and drove off like he was trying to hide something." "Naturally, I followed him," Donoho said. "When it looked like I couldn't overtake him, I fired into the air. At this, he began to throw gallon jugs from his car into the street." Donoho said he shot the right tire out as Nichols turned the corner at Eighth Avenue and Taylor Street, but it failed to halt the car. "At Ninth and Garland, I shot his left rear tire," Donoho said. "By this time, he had thrown five jugs into the street. At Tenth and Garland, he stopped his car and jumped out with his hands high in the air." Nichols cried, "Lordy, Lordy, do not shoot. I give up." The accuracy of Donoho's shots had frightened the young man. Nichols was charged with reckless driving and breaking glass in the street. He posted a $50 bond on each charge.

Running illegal whiskey helped foster Sgt. Donoho's interest in racing. As head of the debunked Vice Squad, Donoho had set up his presence in Nashville so that many were very afraid of Donoho and other members of the police department. Of the many tavern raids, Donoho had created a network of connections with the owners of the taverns and houses of ill repute. Now that the Vice Squad had been disbanded, Donoho had even greater control of positioning himself as a "protector" of these illegal ventures for a "fee."

Donoho used his connections within the police department to capitalize on the use of police threats of raids and intimidation. Black and other minority establishments were seen as easy targets. Charges including drunkenness, vagrancy, and loitering sent clear messages to law violators. Officers picked up a large quantity of untaxed whiskey from them. They also relieved several patrons of ice picks, knives, and pistols. In one place, the raid broke up a dice game. There were also 13 women arrested on clinic law crackdowns. 'Clinic Law' violations referred to women accused of spreading sexually transmitted diseases, usually through prostitution. Women, in particular, were easily targeted, whether actively breaking the law or not. In Nashville, prostitution houses were typical. Law enforcement could charge any woman of violating the Clinic Law under a law during World War I and World War II titled "American Plan," if she were suspected of carrying infectious diseases or STDs. The practice of arresting women under this suspicion was common and often abused by law enforcement as an intimidation tactic.

10. The Crooks Strike Back

"Adam did not want the apple for the apple's sake; he wanted it because it was forbidden."
– Mark Twain

Law enforcement was often the target of threats by criminals. My great-uncle assisted in apprehending two men charged with a plot to kill Policeman R. C. Shoemate. Courtroom testimony described the incident and how Sgt. Donoho assisted in the investigation and arrest of two men believed to have made the threat against Officer Shoemate's life. The suspects, Brownie Thomas Hickam and Lane Montgomery, were charged with carrying a pistol, loitering on the street, and assault and battery. Both were later freed on bond. The incident occurred around 3 a.m. on Gallatin Road as Shoemate drove home from work. It came less than a week after Shoemate's life was threatened by a note left in East Park near a crudely built fiery cross.

The penciled threat stemmed from a disturbance. Earlier, Shoemate previously shot Lounes "Slick" Wilburn, who was 21. In this place, criminal activity was common. Officer Shoemate had been ordered to clean up the area. On his way home from work, the plot to kill Shoemate was overheard and reported to the police. Shoemate testified to details of how Sgt. Donoho used his personal car to follow Officer Shoemate. Donoho stayed two blocks behind, driving with lights out. "As I went out Gallatin Road," Shoemate said. "I saw this convertible parked in a filling station at Calvin Avenue. I saw both men look at me. They started their car after I passed and fell in behind me."

The other car continued down Gallatin Road. He said the vehicle was about twenty-five feet behind his when he turned it off. Donoho then stopped the vehicle, and Shoemate drove back to Gallatin Road. Sgt. Morgan Smith was also in the neighborhood at the time and reported that a .38 Caliber Spanish revolver containing two cartridges was found in the car's glove compartment, and a club was lying on the seat. "The men said they had no intention of harming Shoemate," the officer said. "And that they just happened to be following his car." Neither Hickam nor Montgomery testified. Shoemate testified that he had not seen either of the suspects during the disturbance in East Park. "They made no effort to harm you, did they?" questioned Attorney Taylor. "No," replied Shoemate. "If they had, they wouldn't be here now because they would have been killed." Taylor contended the police had no right to stop the car. "They can't wait until an officer gets killed to do something," Shoemate stated. Wilburn, the youth wounded in the East Park shooting, had been dismissed from General Hospital. He was shot in the lower abdomen, arm, and leg. Shoemate said he fired on Wilburn after he grabbed the officer's nightstick and threatened him, saying "he'd make me eat it." Shoemate said Wilburn was one of several people arrested because they were creating a disturbance at the corner of South Seventh and Russell Streets. The threatening note left by the flaming cross was signed "The Gang" and bore a rough sketch of a skull.

****

Officers were often victims of crime. This was the case with my great-uncle, whose home was burglarized. Thieves ransacked the home of Police Sgt. Donoho. On Saturday night, they stole six pistols from his prized target gun collection. Donoho reported that a "Collection of Pistols" was stolen. In addition to the pistols, the burglars took three watches, Mrs. Donoho's engagement ring and wedding band, and some pistol ammunition and gauges. Some of the guns were loaded. "And they even took my boy's piggy banks," Donoho reported.

The same thieves broke into a neighboring home owned by Lloyd Smith on Coleman Lake Road, stealing 20-25 silver dollars, a gold piece, and two watches. Officers from the sheriff's office, city police, R. R. Poe (Chief of the privately owned Montague-Madison Police Force), and Inglewood-Madison police investigated the theft. Donoho appraised his guns at about $1,000. Donoho, a champion sharpshooter, stated that he would not have sold the pistols for $1,000 as he had begun collecting the pistols around 15 years earlier. He reiterated that the thieves should be glad no one was home. Mrs. Donoho is an expert marksman, winning the lady's shoot in the Tennessee-Mississippi Shoot three times. With their accurate shooting skills, either Mr. or Mrs. Donoho could have easily taken the thieves out.

Many law enforcement officials were loyal to Donoho and offered their help. Warden James E. Edwards of the state prison sent bloodhounds to try to track the burglars. Donoho offered monetary rewards for information leading to the arrest and conviction of the criminals.

11. Promoted to Inspector

"The police are the public, and the public are the police; the police being only members of the public who are paid to give full-time attention to duties which are incumbent on every citizen in the interests of community welfare and existence."

– Robert Peel

In November 1956, Police Sgt. Carney A. Patterson and Sgt. Bill Donohoe's ranks were boosted to Police Inspectors. Six promotions were announced in the department. Donoho's work with the Vice Squad raids, notoriety in the American Legion, and involvement in bringing Stockcar Racing to Nashville Fairgrounds Speedway meant that Bill Donoho was very busy.

Inspector Donoho showed off his shooting skills in May 1957 when he shot a 28-year-old suspect in the left leg while he tried to flee from officers. The suspect took officers on a half-block run from Layman's Drug Store. Inspector Donoho was called to a break-in at the drug store and found the suspect inside. The suspect – John William Terrell Jr. – was taken to General Hospital and charged with housebreaking and theft.

Nashville Police Inspector Donoho has had his fair share of interesting and unique police chases, from having to drive a peddler's wagon early in his police career to shooting escaped cows and/or bulls that ran through the streets of Nashville. In 1958, it was a 1000-pound

Hereford that unsuccessfully attempted to escape from Union Stockyards. Donoho killed the bull with a single shotgun slug after a two-hour chase involving more than 16 men. Incidentally, this bull was Donoho's 12th since 1948, and he shot it firing one-handed while driving across Park Green at 30 miles an hour.

The political thermometer heated within the Nashville Police Department. Dissention and division becoming increasingly splintered made the Nashville Police Department a spectacle in the 1960s. Fighting to move through the cracked department within the public eye grew wider as the tug of war for power within the department stretched into their respective corners. Some of the divisions occurred due to policy changes that Police Chief D.E. Hosse made within the department. Some of the changes included standardizing the pistols given to officers and lowering the presence of police by forcing the normal two-by-two beat per area down to only one officer per area. The officers saw this as a threat to officer safety, as well as the safety of the citizens. This sent a clear message to law violators. A police presence, or lack of police presence, allowed laws to be violated with no one to corroborate the dirty deeds. Citizens of Nashville became prime targets.

Police Chief Hosse defended both of his decisions because he felt they provided better basic police operations. There was unquestionable evidence of contention among the top brass. For some time, one high official was assigned to supervise car maintenance. During the March 31 primary, Police Chief Douglas Hosse and Inspector Carney Patterson had a run-in at the precinct in the City Office building. Chief Hosse reportedly touched Patterson's shoulders and shook him at a high exchange point. The dispute allegedly stemmed from the chief's belief that the forces of candidate Leslie Jett had mobilized to carry the election. Chief Hosse, Mayor Ben West, and other segments of the city administration supported the other candidate. However, Jett, who won an overwhelming victory, had substantial support in the department where his brother, Willard Jett, was a highly regarded Inspector.

Chief Hosse quickly said he became the first police chief in modern history to be voted off the Police Benefit Associations' Board of Directors. Hoss says he was voted off because he wanted to tighten up benefits to ensure a sounder operation of the association. Others who were dropped were Bill Donoho, Inspector; Frank Graves, Sergeant-at-arms of the city council; and R. W. Hamby, a detective. Assistant Chief Frank Muller was elected association president by the new board.

Officers say that Sgt. Underwood's leadership on the ticket reflects the feelings of officers that Sgt. Underwood had not been treated fairly. Others saw a sort of repudiation of the city administration not getting elected, and that some of those considered 'out of grace' did get elected. Reports were that Inspector Donoho made an investigation to determine just who in his detail voted against him. Donoho reportedly conducted a little detective work within the department. Those who voted against him found themselves shifted to different assignments. Some went from patrol duty to inside jobs. Whether this was a routine switch or not was the subject of much speculation. City Patrolman Joe D. Casey, who coached the police team in the Babe Ruth Baseball League to sixth place nationally last year, was relieved of his coaching assignment. He also supported Jett. Another patrolman who backed Jett – William J Barnes – was reportedly ordered to take shotgun firing practice for 20 days. The behind-the-scenes maneuvering in the police department continued during a time when superiors attempted to teach their subordinates courtesy and loyalty. Chief Hosse told a city council committee that the theme of civility only runs through the police training schools.

12. More Arrests

"Lying and stealing are next door neighbors."
– Proverb

Early in 1961, a teenage server was arrested on her first wedding anniversary for faking a $600 holdup with her brother and another man at the restaurant where she worked. The girl–Mrs. Adrian West, 17–and the two men were charged with grand larceny. She was placed in Juvenile Detention Quarters. In City Jail, also charged with grand theft, were Riley King, 25, and Harold Thomason, 22. Police Inspector Donoho stated that Mrs. West admitted to the faked robbery, which included a real punch on the jaw in the restaurant. Mrs. West had previously refused to join the plot with the two men, but when they appeared at the restaurant early and offered her a third of the money, the girl agreed. At 3:45 am, the girl notified police of an armed robbery at the restaurant. Donoho, Sgt. John B. Kittrell, and Patrolman Joe Casey went to the restaurant. Mrs. West stated that a man robbed her of nearly $50 at gunpoint, hitting her in the jaw and knocking her unconscious. "Her brother had punched her," Donoho said, "then, to make it look even better, she scratched her cheek with her fingernail, so it bled." Donoho stated that Mrs. West "put on a real act." But she calmed down so quickly and completely that he became suspicious. He said that within an hour of the time the holdup was reported, Mrs. West had signed a statement admitting the hoax. Around 9 a.m., Donoho and the other officers found the two thieves at their associate's home and arrested them.

Inspector Donoho continued to be active as he made more arrests in Nashville. He arrested and jailed another teenager on seven counts of auto theft in a cops-and-robber type chase at speeds of more than 70 miles per hour. Jerry Lynn Jernigan, 18, was taken into custody after wrecking a stolen car as he ran from police. The chase started when Inspector Donoho and Patrolman Kenneth Reasonover spotted Jernigan in a stolen car. Jernigan lost control of the vehicle near 10th Avenue N and Harrison Avenue. Jernigan wrecked the car, then abandoned it with police in hot pursuit. Jernigan fell headlong down a railroad embankment, cutting his nose and mouth substantially. Donoho said the youth admitted to stealing six other cars. He was also charged with four cases of leaving the scene of an accident and four cases of reckless driving when he wrecked four of the stolen cars. Donoho said, "The boy would just steal the cars, drive them awhile until he wrecked them or thought he was being chased." Four of the cars were recovered in the vicinity of 8th Avenue N and Charlotte Avenue, Donoho said. The others were found wrecked and scattered about the city. The trial for Jernigan was set for later that year.

In July 1961, Police Inspector Bill Donoho and Sgt. Oscar Stone destroyed two slot machines that had been confiscated in a raid. Cigarette smoke had drawn the police to two slot machines hastily locked in a cabinet in the restaurant. Donoho said the cigarettes had been left in ashtrays beside the machines by patrons of the Flame Room, 2612 Jefferson Street, who had been playing the one-armed bandits only moments before. As police entered the restaurant at 3 a.m., the patrons fled. Somebody slammed shut and locked the cabinet doors containing the slot machines. But the cigarettes burned on, and smoke curled from the cabinet. Seeing it, the raiding officers broke open the cabinet and confiscated the devices. The officers found $249.05 in cash hidden near a dice table. The slot machines also contained money. Otis "Pee Wee" Carter, the operator of the Flame Room, was arrested on charges of operating a slot machine, a dice game, a disorderly house, and possessing whiskey for resale. Carter did not appear for his City Court trial and forfeited $50 on each of the five counts—$250. Judge Andrew Doyle ordered the money from the dice game, and the slot machines turned over to the City Welfare Fund. It came to $338.13. One of the slot machines contained $49.25 in quarters. The other had $34.80 in nickels and three pennies someone used to try to cheat the machine. Two cases of whiskey confiscated in the raid were turned over to the state. Donoho and Sgt. Stone smashed the slot machines.

Acting Police Chief Frank Muller gave a 30-day suspension to a city patrolman who cursed a superior officer after trying to crash the gate at the Fairgrounds Speedway, whose President was Inspector Bill Donoho. Patrolman George Kidwell was suspended July 8, the day after the incident at the Fairgrounds Speedway. Suspensions within the department were becoming commonplace. The new regime, which was early in its development, had taken notice and decided to strengthen the department by forcing individual officers to strictly abide by a code of ethics. This brought total suspensions to 12 in the Nashville Police Department since Police Chief Frank Muller became the Acting Chief. Mayor Ben West told him to tighten up police department discipline. In a letter to the Civil Service Commission, Muller gave this account of the incident for which Patrolman Kidwell was suspended. "Kidwell, with his wife and daughter, approached the ticket seller at the Nashville Speedways and purchased a ticket each for his wife and daughter. Upon advancing to the ticket taker, he attempted to gain admission for himself on presentation of his badge." He was informed by the ticket taker that all uniformed police and passes were admitted only at the pass gate. Kidwell took issue with the ticket taker and became angry and cursed. Police were called, and upon Inspector Donoho's arrival, he cursed Inspector Donoho and refused to go with the inspector to the pass gate. Kidwell continued his obscene remarks. After it was impossible to reason with Patrolman Kidwell, Inspector Donoho told him he was suspended from duty. Donoho, in addition to his police job, was working the track the night of the incident. Ultimately, Acting Chief Muller suspended the patrolman for conduct unbecoming an officer.

13. Asst. Chief/Another Track

"Does the plain, simple beauty of life get buried under society's so-called required daily activities or is that just true of me? No, I know I'm not alone in that feeling. We all get caught up in the making and spending of money. I know it's not just me."
— Dan Groat, An Enigmatic Escape: A Trilogy

Bill Donoho, Bennie Goodman, and Mark Parrish–owners of Nashville's Fairgrounds Speedway since 1958–completed the purchase of Birmingham's Dixie Speedway for a reported price of $100,000. The purchase was made from Dixie Auto Racing Enterprises, which listed owners Eddie Wright, Bartow Brown, and Earl Roberts. John Simmons of Birmingham was immediately appointed as the general manager of operations. Goodman served as general manager of the Nashville Track. The Dixie Speedway was regarded as one of the country's finest quarter-mile, banked asphalt ovals and has a seating capacity of 4,200. For the owners, Goodman said, "We believe the Dixie Speedway has not been operated to its potential and that it is one of the best tracks in the land. This area has a large population, and we believe that with some changes, we can put Birmingham auto racing on a real money-making level." Negotiations for the deal had been ongoing since November 1961. Goodman reported that this would not affect racing in Nashville, and that this season's program would go as scheduled. He hinted there might be more intercity rivalry between racers from the two cities, and added, "This would be good for auto racing fans at both tracks." Donoho, Goodman, and Parrish had a new quarter mile added to the local speedway. The half-mile track was resurfaced. Plans called for the track to be rebuilt. Crowds had increased each year since the speedway opened, and 115,800 fans turned out to watch the rapidly growing sport in 1961.

In January 1963, Newspaper Headlines touted, "Donoho in Line for Promotion, Head of Services and Expected to be Assistant Police Chief." Bill Donoho, Chief of Services for the Nashville Police Department, was reportedly in line for the post of Assistant Chief of Police, which was vacated in February by Assistant Chief Carney Patterson. Donoho had to be rated among the top three officers taking the Civil Services Examination to get the position. Two other candidates also applied for the job. The four division chiefs, along with all inspectors with five or more years of service in their posts, were eligible to take the exam given by the Nashville Civil Services Commission. Donoho related to news media that he would take the exam. Mayor Ben West appointed the position to the officer with the highest ranking on the test. Mayor West had stated publicly that the job was Donoho's, if his scores were high enough, so he had mayoral support. Attorney Willis West, the Mayor's brother, is said to have played a part in the selection during recent meetings.

If chosen, Donoho's salary would increase to $7,980 per year. Retiring Assistant Chief Carney Patterson would receive 50% of his current salary for the rest of his life. Asst. Chief

Patterson had 28 years of service with the Davidson County Police Department and was promoted to Assistant Chief in January 1962. This promotion allowed Patterson to retire at higher pay. Although he said his plans were indefinite, the policy would enable him to earn money elsewhere as well as Mayor West supported Donoho, even though the two were reported to have had a disagreement several years earlier when Donoho refused to sell his interest in an automobile racing track. Ultimately, Inspector Donoho was chosen and promoted to Assistant Police Chief.

14. Undercover/Retirement

"The sweeter the apple, the blacker the core."
— *Dorothy Parker*

Civil Service charges were placed against four suspended city police officers charged with offenses ranging from moonshine whiskey operations to taking pictures without ascertainable authority in Printer's Alley. This information came to light when Assistant Chief Bill Donoho explained to a group of East Nashville residents why the protection against the rash of muggings in that area had not improved. The citizens were moved to action by the recent attack on an aged babysitter, who subsequently died, and the failure of city police to answer a plea to aid in the search after the woman was reported missing. Police Chief Frank Muller investigated this incident and cleared the department of any negligence. Since then, the patrol was doubled in East Nashville. Assistant Chief Donoho had to stand before an outraged group and admit that four "bad apples" in the department were going before the board. Apples do rot, but not without cause. In an administration where high-ranking police officers were used too much as political ward heelers, poll watchers, or babysitters, it was a small wonder that the spoilage rate of junior officers was high. Too many bad apples turned up. With the coming of the new Metropolitan government, it was time to examine the tree. It was time that leaders of Metro consider planting a whole new orchard.

On March 12, 1963, Donoho made headlines again, when the Nashville City Council honored him for saving the city money. The Council presented Bill Donoho, City Police Chief of Services, with a Citation honoring him for the work he had done. The Resolution said Donoho initiated a program that saved Nashville approximately $12,500 a year in maintenance costs for patrol cars. Instead of buying entirely new emergency units each year, Donoho developed a program to overhaul the five units, saving about $2,500 on each one. City Council recognized the Resolution honoring Donoho.

On March 19, 1963, Bill Donoho, Assistant Police Chief, visited two physicians, stating that these appointments were merely routine. Bill Donoho said when asked that he had no intention of requesting a disability pension soon, but said he had thought about it. Donoho made the statement amid reports that he planned to retire from the police department only days after he had been promoted from Chief of Services to the Assistant Chief post. Donoho's pension, if he requested one, would be based on his present salary as Assistant Chief, even though he served for less than two weeks. "They're just rumors," the police chief said. "I've been hearing those reports myself." Donoho had recently visited his physician Dr. Paul G Morrissey Jr., but denied it had anything to do with pension plans. He also saw Dr. W. J. Core, the County Medical Examiner, two weeks earlier for a routine physical checkup. Dr. Core needed to examine all persons requesting disability pensions; the doctor then made recommendations to the Civil Service

Commission. "This was all just a coincidence," Donoho exclaimed when pressed. A few days later, more reports circulated that other superior officers, requesting they be placed on pension. Others requested pensions based on years of service. Dr. Core stated that his examination of Donoho two weeks previously disclosed that the officer suffered from an arthritic spine. As for pension, Donoho apparently would have to have his request approved on the spinal ailment.

****

The brutal beatings and robbery of Mrs. Hattie Harris, 75-year-old babysitter, set off one of the most unusual operations in Nashville Police history. Police Chief Frank Muller was out of town. Finding the assailant fell to Donoho, recently named acting assistant chief. "We intend to catch whoever did this," Donoho stated. He called a conference to talk to his senior officers. This was Donoho's idea: four officers would be dressed as women. They would walk the East Nashville area to draw the killer into making a play. "I reviewed files of the last six similar cases, all of which had happened in the previous two months," Donoho stated. "All the victims were elderly women. They had all been beaten, robbed, or molested."

The men went to work. Harvey's Clothing Store donated women's clothing. A beauty shop donated wigs for the officers. Men were selected for the job. They were various sizes, but all weighed under 100 pounds and could pass easily for women, at least in dim light. The day after Mrs. Harris was assaulted, police were ready. Mrs. Harris died the next day of her injuries. Those who lived in East Nashville were gripped by fear. Charles Mills, Brodie Pruitt, Donald Dozier, and Robert A. Green dressed and started their assignment. This operation began in January 1963, and ended in March 1963. The men operated between First and Tenth Streets, Shelby, and Main Streets–in all, 40 blocks. They walked two blocks apart, and help was only minutes away. Ten officers were assigned full-time to the case, in addition to two detectives, traffic patrol officers, and regular police officers assigned to the East Nashville beats. The Female garb prompted one of the officers to remark, "I don't see how women stand it with all that cold air whipping under their skirts." However, the weird patrols got results, although not always the ones expected. Once, a pedestrian in the area approached homicide Officer Charles L. Stoner, standing nearby in plain clothes. "Are you a police officer?" he asked. Stoner said he was. "Well, I want to report something," the man said. "I just saw the ugliest woman I have ever seen walking down the street. She was so ugly I was not even sure she was a woman. I wish you would investigate." Trying hard to keep a straight face, Stoner said he would, indeed, investigate. The 'ugly woman' was Detective Mills.

The men went out every night except when it was snowing, raining, or sub-zero temperatures. Numerous times men tried to pick them up or offer them rides. Once, a preacher circled the block four times, eyeing one of the officers. On the fourth time, he pulled his car into an alley before the disguised police officer and stopped. The officer jumped behind the car and took the license number. The surprised preacher took off. He was brought in for questioning the next day, and he told the police he did not know why he had done it. He was released. The men were well prepared for whatever might come. In the right pocket of the officer's coat, each carried a .38 snub-nosed revolver. In their left pocket were a flashlight and police whistle. The men also had tiny 11-ounce walkie-talkies for instant communication with nearby patrol cars. The phony women walked their rounds from 5:30 pm until after midnight. Then they would change clothes and follow up on any leads or reports they had obtained. During the time the disguises were used, several suspects were brought to police headquarters for questioning, many of them as a result of the night walkers. Others were questioned elsewhere. On the first night of the experiment, an officer reported 18 or 20 attempts to pick him up. For two of the officers, the assignment struck close to home. Detective Lynn Bowers' grandmother, Mrs. Hazel Ford, 63, had been knocked down and robbed of money and groceries on December 26 as she returned from the store. A cook who worked in a boarding house run by Detective Bill Stinnett's wife was also knocked down and robbed in New York-style muggings.

However, by early February, the disguises began to wear thin. People in the neighborhood, especially children, recognized the officers and called to them as they made their rounds. The disguises gradually outlived their usefulness. Officer Green felt he had had a close call. As he walked down Shelby Street, three boys, walking fast, followed him and got directly behind him.

At that point, a police car came down the street, and the three boys ran ahead. "They had something in mind," Green said. "I'm not sure what." Once, a woman from Chattanooga pulled her car over and asked two of the disguised officers what they were doing all dressed up, and said she had a mind to call the police. On another occasion, a woman passed the officers on the sidewalk, stopped, and said, "Ladies, you had better watch out. You can get killed out here." Bowers said six or eight cases were reported in the area over the last several months. The women were all beaten and robbed. All the cases showed a similar pattern. "We're still working on this case," Muller said. And if the disguises did not catch Mrs. Harris' killer, they gave the participating officers insight into problems in the East Nashville area. Some felt that their presence, although widely known, was enough to deter a repetition of the victim's attack.

15. Under Suspicion

"The revolution is not an apple that falls when it is ripe. You have to make it fall."
— *Che Guevara*

Nashville's police department had been deeply scarred by years of scandal and political hanky-panky. The inauguration of the Metropolitan Government signaled the end of the city's ever-recurring police problems. The need for a department change had never been greater. Indications were strong with a stand taken by Metro Mayor-elect Beverly Briley. The new mayor had grand plans for cleaning up the department from top to bottom. The retirement of some 25 police officers, most of whom bitterly fought against adopting the Metropolitan Government, left Briley with a free hand in forging a new police force. Many of those who took their pensions were from top police echelons, including the police chief, two assistant police chiefs, two other department heads, four inspectors, and two lieutenants. Those who retired included Police Chief Frank W. Muller, Sr. Assistant Chief Carney Patterson, and Assistant Chief "Wild Bill" Donoho who took Patterson's vacated post for a month. The only people left in the top six positions were Hubert O. Kemp, traffic chief, and Braxton M. Duke, Chief of services, who were both strong supporters of Briley.

Most of those who returned opposed Metro, consistently trying to restrict the new government. Mayor-elect Briley has vowed to appoint men to the positions who will restore dignity to the police profession in Davidson County. Mayor-elect Briley launched a platform he hoped would provide the police department with a new image. The scandals associated with individuals in the police department scarred all law enforcement. Each police department's wrong-doings, large or small, adds to a long and ever-increasing list of incidents that weakened public confidence in the men in blue.

Accusations by the police chief against Inspector Morgan Smith and others of making bonds for suspects arrested during the operation of the Oranges Inn prompted new rules. The rule prohibited police personnel from making bonds for any arrested person. Three months earlier, Smith posted bond for bondsman Jake Rader, charged with shooting fellow bondsman Robert Widdey. Police Chief H. O. Kemp suspended Inspector Smith. In defense, the sergeant stated that he had "never heard" of the bond-making rule. Kemp gave Smith his choice of being fired or taking his pension. Smith took his retirement with his pension. Bill Donoho took his disability pension in March 1963, only days after being promoted from Chief of Services to Assistant Chief of Police. When he retired, his pension was based on the salary of an Assistant Chief, although he had served in that position only a few days. Suspicion of criminal activity within the new department went back to the 1950s. Those under investigation for crimes included Officer Morgan Smith, Assistant Police Chief Bill Donoho, former Sheriff Leslie Jett, and several others.

16. A Letter to Wild Bill

History of Federal Prison Camp at Montgomery, Alabama

The Bureau of Prisons has had many achievements and overcome several challenges. On May 14, 1930, Congress created the Bureau of Prisons within the Department of Justice. The agency was responsible for the management and regulation of all three penitentiary establishments. The wardens functioned autonomously. However, wardens were under the supervision of a DOJ official, the Superintendent of Prisons, in Washington, DC. More federal prisons were created to help with the growing crime within the country.

July 1, 1968

My Dearest Bill,

Time seems to have stopped. Watching you walk through the prison gates this afternoon made me question our life together. How could people believe that you, "a pillar of everything that is good and right in this world," could deserve a fate like this? My emotions have bubbled over as I've tried to comprehend our government's actions. I realize that moving forward is in the best interest of our family, especially Jim, but it's really hard. It is hard. It is hard being without you. Jim misses you. I just do not understand.

Don and Henry Lee were at the house when I returned home. They scampered about angrily throughout the house, but when Jim came in, their tones softened. The injustice that has plagued our family is just plain incomprehensible. Everyone that knows us says so. This was a blatant attack by a political regime that needed to throw their weight around so that the Metro government could somehow establish control. You were a small fish in a big pond; examples had to be made by the men who made Nashville great.

I have complained enough about this situation. Just know that your brothers are helping me keep an eye on our business interests. We will overcome this nightmare. Jim and I love you so much, and we cannot wait to see you home. I pray they are treating you well. John [Hooker] has assured us that time will move by quickly. I hate the idea of missing the holidays with you. Thanksgiving, your birthday, and Christmas celebrations will forever have new meanings to us.

Always yours,
Jessie Mildred (your Maude)

Bill read and re-read his wife's letter as he sat quietly waiting. The dread was actually upon him. The processing, body searches, and aloneness in this abhorrent place seemed to envelop his entire body. Memories of the tears in his wife's eyes as guards took him away were a pain almost too hard to bear. He hoped Jim was comforted by his uncles. His eyes watered; he wiped his cheek, sighed deeply, and curled up on the bed, hoping that sleep would come sooner than later.

Following a routine had never been an issue. He had always prided himself on rising early each morning, drinking his coffee with his breakfast, and catching up on the day's news in *The Tennessean*. He had run his day at the top of a clock, always following a regimented schedule mostly of his own choosing. Being in prison was regimented, but not of his own choosing. No longer being in control of what he did, and when he did it was a hard pill to swallow.

He was grateful that his attorney's connections negotiated the plan for him to serve his time out of state, so it took some pressure off the Fairgrounds Speedway. Bill didn't want his confinement to slow down his legacy of the Nashville Fairgrounds Speedways. Bennie and Mark would take care of everything. Don and Henry Lee would see to it that things ran smoothly at home. Bill had always counted on his younger brothers to be supportive and protective. After all, that is what family does for one another, right?

Frustration, anger, and resentment seethed in Bill's heart. The government had treated him like a mob boss, Al Capone-style. He felt betrayed. It was impossible to prove his innocence when the judge's bias refused to allow evidence that supported his case. His thoughts wandered. Attorney General Merrick needed a career case. And apparently, creating a case against Donoho using evil characters such as William Frazier and Lula Grey against him was the best the government could do. He had time to figure out what and how this happened. He would prioritize his thoughts on building a future for his son.

17. Trials (Part 1)

"I am sometimes a fox and sometimes a lion. The whole secret of government lies in knowing when to be the one or the other."
— *Napoleon Bonaparte*

October 7, 1964, the government called 20 witnesses to testify in an income tax fraud case against former Assistant Police Chief Bill Donoho, attempting to prove his expenditures exceeded his tax-reported earnings. Real estate transactions, automobile purchases, bank accounts, and purchases of clothing and furniture were among the items detailed by government witnesses. Donoho pled innocent to the five-count indictment that charged him with perjury in filing a false income tax return for 1957, 1958, and 1962. The government based its case on the 1960 and 1961 expenditures. U.S. District Judge Frank Gray Jr., the presiding judge, refused to permit a government witness to testify about the availability of alleged payoffs until the prosecution had laid a foundation. The jury was excused from the courtroom when Kilgore called Jimmy Ray Payne of Nashville, a former blackjack dealer, to testify. Kilgore said he wanted to show that Payne had witnessed payoff to police officers but not to Donoho. He said Payne would testify that he had contributed to a payoff fund. Defense Attorney John J. Hooker Sr. protested that the testimony would be "highly prejudicial" to the defendant and should not be permitted. Among witnesses testifying concerning Donoho's bank accounts earnings and expenditures were:

– Harold J. Castner, First American National Bank, testified Donoho had a savings account balance on December 31, 1959, of $13,285.85; a balance of $15,455.17 at the end of 1960; and $22,108.58 at the end of 1961. His wife, Mrs. Mildred Donoho, had checking account balances for the same years of $73.79, 98.20, and $40.97.

– Hayes Graft, Third National Bank, who testified that Mrs. Donoho had an account with that bank under the name of Mrs. Jessie M. Donoho, with a balance at the end of 1959 of $1,678.11, $1,728.82 at the end of 1960, and $981.05 at the end of 1961.

– William Bower, First Federal Savings and Loan Association, testified William J. Donoho had savings account balances of $7,315.88, $7,237.88, and 11,930.06 at the end of the years 1959, 1960, and 1961.

– Charles Buchannan Jr., custodian of Metropolitan government payroll records, testified that Donoho was paid $249.17 twice monthly in 1960 and 1961 with fewer withholdings.

– William O. Lee, Guaranty Title Co., testified concerning the purchase by Donoho in May 1961 of property at Tenth and Russell streets for $7,500.

October 29, 1965, Newspaper Headlines courted a picture of Bill Donoho with a sensationalized caption headline that read "Donoho Sanity Court Question." U.S. District Court was asked to determine if the former Assistant Police Chief Bill Donoho was mentally competent to stand trial after receiving a report stating that he had "suicidal tendencies." U.S. Attorney James F. Neal stated in a motion that John E. Mask, special agent for the Internal Revenue Services, had filed a report of his interview with Dr. Paul Morrissey Jr., one of Donoho's physicians. Neal said Agent Mask reported that Dr. Morrissey's records "recorded suicidal tendencies in the defendant." Officer Mask and Attorney Neal reported that Morrissey "had advised the defendant, Donoho, to seek psychiatric aid." Attorney Neal said this information and a previous letter from Morrissey concerning Donoho's health "constituted reasonable cause to believe that the defendant may be so mentally incompetent as to be unable to assist in his own defense properly." Attorney Neal asked the court to commit Mr. Donoho to a mental institution designated by the court to determine his mental competency. The Honorable Judge Miller declined to commit Donoho but did order Donoho to submit to a psychiatric evaluation.

Dr. Otto Billig, a Nashville psychiatrist, stated in his letter to Judge Miller he saw Donoho "for psychiatric evaluation on April 15, 1966, and completed psychological testing on May 10, 1966." Dr. Otto Billig said Donoho dates the "onset of his illness to June 1965, when he developed diabetes and high blood pressure." However, over the following two years, Donoho had become increasingly "shaky" and had become more and more forgetful as to dates and had developed anxiety that has manifested in the forms of feelings of apprehension, feeling jittery, feeling dizzy, having heart palpitations, and respiratory difficulties. These attacks last approximately 30 minutes and re-occur at irregular intervals, from daily to about two or three times weekly. The doctor also stated that Donoho had "sleep disturbances." "And he worries a great deal about the effect of his legal difficulties on his family, particularly on his only son." After further detailing Donoho's condition, Dr. Billig concluded that the former policeman suffered from anxiety reactions due to emotional stress. However, this anxiety, he said, "does not interfere with his ability to comprehend the charges against him, and he believed that Donoho can properly assist in the preparation of his defense." Dr. Billig added that Donoho's anxiety reactions were likely to continue "as long as the stressful situation exists." U.S. Attorney Gilbert S. Merritt Jr. said that he anticipated the case would move forward and now go to trial. Dr. Billig stated that Mr. Donoho "had become very much concerned about his difficulties reflecting on his own, and admitted to having contemplated suicide but denies any real suicidal intentions since this too would have adverse effects on his son."

Government officials stated in open court that Donoho had paid $5,000 for promotions. Lt. R. B. Owen, called as a government rebuttal witness, told the jury that Donoho has a "corrupt" character, his name was "not good," and that he had a reputation for "not telling the truth." Owen made this statement in response to questions asked by U.S. Attorney Merritt. Incidentally, to this author, the testimony about Sgt. Smith receiving payoffs from Mr. Krietner and reporting to the court officials that Smith said half would go to Chief Donoho would be considered hearsay.

Donoho, meanwhile, denied that he paid $5,000 to an unidentified city official for a promotion to police inspector. The defendant further denied that he paid $500 to former councilman Charlie Riley to obtain a job on the Nashville Police Force, and even denied knowing Charlie Riley; however, he did add that the late Tony Sudekum got him his job on the police force. Donoho met Sudekum when he first moved to Nashville as a barber, stating that Tony Sudekum, a regular client, had volunteered to help him obtain employment with the Nashville Police Department.

There were three alleged law violators who testified: Lula Gray, who testified that she ran a house of prostitution, stated under oath that she paid Donoho $150 a month from August 1957 through August 1958; William Bill Frazier, a Nashville gambler, testified under oath that he paid Donoho $100 monthly for five years beginning in 1957; and Albert "Mickey" Krietner, another "law violator," testified he made protection payments to Sgt. Morgan Smith, formerly of the Nashville police force, for $600 for each year 1957 and 1958, and Smith told Kreitner that Donoho would receive half of those payments. Many accusations were made concerning Donoho's behavior, motives, and actions during the course of his career.

Closing arguments by Donoho's attorney John J. Hooker Sr. were passionately expressed, questioning the jurors. "Whose word are you going to take, this man (pointing at Donoho) who has served you all his life, or people like those law violators (already convicted criminals) who testified for the government?" Hooker then listed the names of the government's witnesses on the blackboard in front of the jury. Donoho's attorney told the jury, "You have just heard government witnesses perjured testimony, foul testimony, and evil people have asked those law violators to testify falsely. Please recognize this deceit."

Attorney Merritt expounded, "Are we to be silenced, stilled in the face of such corruption? Has it come to this that no effort can be made, no hand lifted to prosecute the guilty without it being said that there is a conspiracy to overwhelm the innocent by an all-powerful government? The law violators who came up and testified did not have to do so," said Merritt, adding that "they had nothing to gain. These people are from whom he [pointing at Donoho] took money."

18. Trials (Part 2)

"It is error alone which needs the support of government. Truth can stand by itself."
                    – Thomas Jefferson

For the defense, the members of the old Nashville City Police Department, including former Sgt. Morgan Smith were subpoenaed as defense witnesses. After two days of testimony, the trial of the then 50-year-old retired Assistant Police Chief was halted abruptly due to the illness of U.S. District Judge William Miller. Following this announcement Quentin Housholder, one of Donoho's attorneys, stated that as many as 250 officers may be called to testify. "We think they should have the privilege of denying the charges that they received payoffs; we may subpoena the whole police department." Housholder was referring to the testimony of government witnesses who testified that they paid off as many as 200 officers during the years Donoho was charged with filing false income tax returns. Six admitted law violators testified under oath that they made payoffs to Donoho during the years in question. The government said none of these payments were listed on Donoho's tax returns for these years. Two other law violators were scheduled to testify before the government rested its case. The testimony of at least three of the witnesses was linked to the names of other police officers with alleged payoffs. Among them was Morgan Smith, who recently served a prison term for falsifying income tax returns, former

Police Chief Frank Muller, former Assistant Chief Carney Patterson, Willard Jett, Gordon Vance, and V. A. Bennett, a former constable. Smith, Muller, and Vance were subpoenaed. All the others except Jett, who was out of the state, were expected to testify. Housholder said Inspector Charles Flanders, Sgt. Josh Caney, Sgt. Oscar Stone, all members of the Metro Police Department, former Patrol Chief Oly T. Boner, and Carney Paterson would be among those subpoenaed. Attorney John J. Hooker Sr., Chief Defense Counsel, said it would be up to his client to decide how many former officers were subpoenaed. A list of all officers who were working during the period in question was a substantial number. The calling of Smith came as no surprise, as his name was linked to Donoho by several law violators who had testified. U.S. District Attorney Merritt told the court he intended to prove Smith acted as an "agent" of Donoho in picking up alleged payoffs from the law violators. Smith, an officer for 26 years, was sentenced to 18 months in prison in 1964, after being convicted on three counts of income tax perjury. He was in the witness room when it was announced that the trial would be delayed.

It took several years, several witnesses, and two trials to convict Bill Donoho on charges of receiving over $15,000 in payout money. Skillfully, the District Attorney used Donoho's tax records as evidence. The records did not indicate Donoho's actual income based on the indictment and charges filed. After finally being convicted in November 1966, it was two years before Bill Donoho reported to prison to serve his time. After deliberating only three hours and 20 minutes, William James "Bill" Donoho Sr. was found guilty on five counts.

United States District Attorney Gilbert S. Merritt Jr. worked tirelessly to convince a jury to convict the former Assistant Police Chief Bill Donoho Sr. Donoho was sentenced to fifteen months in federal prison and fined $2,500.00. This statement was the front-page headline on November 2, 1966, in the Nashville *Tennessean*, Nashville's most prominent newspaper. Attorney Merritt stated later that this trial of a law enforcement officer was the most unpleasant legal task he had ever experienced in dealing with the law, but he believed justice had been served. The William "Bill" Donoho case was one of Attorney Gilbert S. Meritt Jr.'s first major cases after becoming the U.S. Prosecutor.

Defense Attorney John J. Hooker Sr. appealed his client's conviction to the U.S. Sixth Circuit Court of Appeals in Cincinnati, Ohio. The appeal was based on 21 alleged errors made during the trial. Hooker alleged that the court refused to do its due diligence for the defendants concerning 15 special requests in presenting the charges to the jury. Hooker further contended that the court erred in declining the defendant's offer of proof by the testimony of a certified public accountant. Donoho's net worth, including his expenditures and receipts of money during the period, was not presented to the jury. Also, he held that the defendant was not entitled to argue before the jury that the government had withdrawn its positions originally taken in the *Bill of Particulars* that a deficiency in Donoho's income taxes for 1960 and 1961 could be sustained by expenditures and disbursements methods of computing the defendant's taxes. Hooker continued, stating that Honorable Judge Gray was not available to witness the testimony of many witnesses and therefore was prevented from observing their "manner and demeanor." This deprived the defendant of "substantial constitutional rights." Two Judges decided the case for the appellate court: Honorable Paul C. Weick, and Honorable Lester L. Cecil, a senior judge for the appellate courts. The appellate court affirmed Donoho's conviction based mainly on the testimony of Lula Gray and William Frazier. The appellate court said the issues were narrow in scope for the jury. The appellate court agreed with the jury in believing the testimony of law violators for police protection and did not believe Donoho's denials. Judge Gray suspended the execution of the sentence for ten days to give Hooker time to file the notice of appeal. If an appeal was not filed within ten days, Donoho would start serving his sentence immediately.

Judge Gray imposed the sentence after overruling a defense motion for a new trial, argued at considerable length by Attorney Hooker and U.S. Attorney Gilbert S. Merritt Jr. "By its verdict, it is apparent that the jury credited the testimony of the law-breaking criminals and disbelieved the testimony of Mr. Donoho." When asked by Judge Gray if he wanted to say anything before the sentence was imposed, Bill Donoho replied: "I am not guilty of taking any graft or payoffs from any of these people," referring to the six law violators who testified at the trial that they paid Donoho upward of $15,000 for protection. "My family and I have always worked for what we have," Donoho said as he stood at the court podium with his Attorneys John J. Hooker, Quentin Housholder, and Ira Parker. Donoho listened intently to the attorneys argue on the motion for a new trial. When the request was overruled, Hooker told Gray, "Mr. Donoho, to my knowledge, and to the general public's knowledge, has been a distinguished police officer and participated in many sensational arrests." "Mr. Donoho was on the police force 24 years; he is a man of the family, an outstanding citizen, and a man of fine character who has never been arrested or convicted of any crime." The defense attorney concluded by saying he hoped that "his honor will see fit to extend him leniency." Donoho could have received up to 15 years imprisonment and $25,000 in fines. Judge Gray sentenced the defendant to 15 months for each of the five counts, but the sentences were to run concurrently. He fined Donoho $500 on each count. This was the second trial for the same offense a year earlier. That trial ended in a mistrial when it was discovered one of the jurors had had income tax difficulties with the government.

Donoho's conviction in the fall of 1966 was on five counts of an indictment charging him with income tax fraud for five years from 1957 through 1962, exclusive of 1959 which was not involved. Following his conviction in the Fall of 1966, Donoho appealed to the U.S. 6th Circuit Court of Appeals. When that court affirmed his conviction, Donoho asked the U.S. Supreme Court to review it. The high court refused to do so. Judge Gray, nevertheless, made the defendant eligible for parole in four months. Ordinarily, when someone is convicted of a crime, they must serve a third of their sentence before coming up for parole consideration. He was fined $2,500–$500 for each count. John J. Hooker Sr. told the court Donoho was prepared to serve his sentence. However, Assistant U.S. Attorney Alfred Knight III opposed any reduction in Donoho's sentence and pleaded to the courts for Donoho to begin serving his sentence immediately. Attorney Knight had argued that Donoho had had a year and a half since his conviction to get his "business affairs in order." Hooker requested a reduction in the sentence to probation. However, U.S. District Judge Frank Gray Jr. overruled the motion for probation. Hooker asserted Donoho had "business matters and commitments which were necessary for him to be able to take care of." Hooker explained that Donoho operated Nashville Speedways, Inc., and May, June, and July were his most profitable months. The attorney said Donoho wanted to procure someone to work the business during his absence. Donoho explained to the court he owned 50% of the business, and five local persons owned the remaining 50%. Hooker handed the court a financial report which reflected the Speedway firm's operations. It was returned to the attorney and not filed as part of the case with the courts. Hooker told the court that Donoho's wife was entirely dependent upon him for support, and his mother, who was 83, was partially reliant on Donoho.

Bill Donoho won an extension of time to Monday, July 1, 1968, in which to begin serving a federal sentence for income tax fraud. Donoho had asked that he be allowed to report on August 1, stating he needed this time to get his affairs in order.

In 1967, the last organized crime cases in Davidson County were disposed of in federal court. U.S. District Judge William E. Miller sentenced the defendants to 18 months and fined them $500. He then suspended the imposition of sentence and placed the gamblers on three years' probation. They were given a week to pay the fine. There were guilty pleas to only one of the seven-count indictments, which charged them with using interstate facilities to order a shipment of dice from Cincinnati, Ohio. G. M. Wallwork, Chief of Intelligence Division, and Internal Revenue Service, were prime leaders in the massive investigation that started in 1962. FBI Agents also participated in the investigation. It led to the conviction of four law enforcement officers and many of Nashville's top gamblers. Operators of two large and luxurious gambling casinos were included in the massive investigation. These two casinos and other major gambling establishments in Nashville were closed. Attorney Jack Norman Sr., who represented two of those indicted, told the court that his clients now operated an A-1 restaurant and no longer engaged in any gambling operations.

The police officers convicted were former Police Sgt. Morgan Smith, former Police Lt. John Kittrell, former Davidson County Sheriff Leslie Jett, along with William "Wild Bill"

Donoho, Sr. All four officers served their prison terms. All except Kittrell were convicted on income tax evasion charges; in the other cases, convictions were evidenced by officers accepting payoffs from law violators. The operators of the former Uptown Dinner Club were convicted of using interstate facilities to conduct a huge gambling enterprise. They appealed their convictions. Their cases were also argued before the U.S. Courts of Appeals Sixth Circuit in Cincinnati, Ohio. The Appellate Courts upheld the convictions. Two other defendants operating a now-closed Automobile Business Club near Bordeaux were also convicted of using interstate facilities to conduct a gambling business. Lastly, a former constable for the county was convicted of income tax evasion, and he also served his time. Prosecutors proudly announced that Nashville was thoroughly cleaned up from organized gambling operations on a big scale. If Davidson County had any organized gambling operations, it was hidden within private clubs. The gambling casinos were effectively taken down. However, it was commonly known that many activities and bookies/number racket operations were still within Nashville.

19. More NASCAR

"Anytime in radio that you can reach somebody on an emotional level, you're really connecting."

– Casey Kasem

All races held at Fairgrounds Speedways were broadcast on WENO radio, 1430 on the dial, as were all major NASCAR Grand National events on the superspeedways. Ed Hamilton of WENO broadcasted the local Tuesday and Saturday programs. At the same time, the station's Don Howser handled the public address system at the Speedways, subbing for Ed when he formerly entered motorcycle races. In addition, WENO would broadcast a sports show at 7:45 am and 4:45 pm each day featuring *Tennessean* sportswriter Tom Powell. Broadcasting the conversations and building up anticipation for the audience served to grow the adrenaline rush that people who love racing crave. Being broadcast live gave people the sense of personally witnessing an energized connection associated with racing. Adrenaline rushes climaxed for Coo Coo Marlin as he drove excitedly on his last lap of the day. It detailed the mechanics who worked tirelessly to change tires and fuel up cars in what seemed to be seconds. A rush for Flookie Buford took the win, pushing himself to victory as he finished the race with the thrill of knowing that once his car rolled to a stop, the excitement of the announcers and the crowd could bear a resemblance to the noise of a rocket launch. Listening to the races gave way to the audience's vision and inspiration. The imaginations of young boys who knew they, too, could grow to become one of the thrill-seekers and adrenaline-junky drivers standing beside beautiful women and large trophies at the end of a race.

If Gene Cato's duties at Speedway Fairgrounds ended with waving checkered, green, and yellow flags, he'd have it made. Still, Cato doubled as the track public relations man and oversaw all maintenance work. It was a fact and evidenced that anybody who knew co-owner Bill Donoho knew Bill oversaw Gene and all aspects of the Speedway. In contrast, he managed the rest of the operations. Bill Donoho was in total control and stood high in the eyes of everyone who worked for the Speedway Fairgrounds. Gene's experience had been varied. Although he had never been a driver, he operated the track service station, ran a track in Huntsville during 1965, and returned to Nashville as an assistant flagger to Forrest Prince. He was noted as having no favorites because he liked to see a different winner every time the checkered flag was dropped. Gene Cato was nice, but the drivers knew better than to cross him. He was known as a loyal, dedicated man. He stuck to his convictions, no matter what the consequences.

In November 1967, the newspaper reported that co-owner Bennie Goodman sold his holdings in the Speedway Fairgrounds to Bill Donoho for $100,000, and immediately indicated that he planned to become part of a group interested in building another Super Speedway in Davidson County. Mr. Goodman cited a "personality conflict" as the main reason for the split. He said he looked forward to providing the people of Nashville and the Midstate area with a recreational complex. Nashville had needed one for several years. The sale ended a partnership that had been in existence since 1952. Another former partner, Mark Parrish, had his interest bought by Donoho and Goodman in 1965. Mr. Parrish purchased the Nashville Dixie Flyers of the Eastern Hockey League. Donoho immediately announced the track would continue its NASCAR-sanctioned operation in 1968 on the quarter miles and half mile banked ovals.

Previously, co-owners Bennie Goodman and Bill Donoho decided that to have things run as smoothly as possible, it should be kept in the family. All the family took part in the Fairground operation, too, as Goodman's wife Jo Ann sold tickets and his son Barry, age 15, handled the communication in the control tower. Donoho provided the most extended list of relatives by starting with his wife, Mildred, as a ticket seller. His son, Jim, drove the PACE car and was a part-time announcer when Don Howser couldn't make it. Mattie Lee Massey, a niece of Donoho, was stationed at the pass gate, and ticket takers included D. E. Donoho, an uncle, Billy Whitley, a nephew, and Henry Donoho, his brother. A niece Deborah Jacobson was the full-time secretary. The concession stands were handled by Mary Helen Donoho, Mary Sue Jones, and Peggy Jones, who were all trusted, valued relatives. As a side note, Billy Whitley was Bill Donoho's namesake. Whitley was nephew to Donoho, and this author's mother's brother. My Great-Uncle Billy would often take all my cousins who were of age to Nashville to see the races in the mid-1970s. I was very young and often became upset because my older brothers were always invited to go the races.

20. Trouble with Cars

"The very essence of a free government consists in considering offices as public trusts, bestowed for the good of the country, and not for the benefit of an individual or a party."
– John C. Calhoun

Senators and Representatives in Washington D. C. voiced trepidations about whether inflation or a monopoly was at play within the automobile industry. The auto industry appeared on fire, with economic indicators offering promising results. The industry claimed production would push eight to nine million cars produced each year. This glowing horizon had one problem. At issue was whether the new models were higher priced, and whether these elevated prices would be inflationary. When Chrysler, who led the mob, committed the indelicacy of announcing that new models would cost more, the White House took alarm and Senator Phillip Hart of Michigan rose on the Senate floor to express his uneasiness. Hart's anti-monopoly subcommittee dove headfirst into the concentration, monopoly control, and administered prices that were passed on to consumers. Soon after, General Motors and Ford announced they were increasing prices. The White House called the Bureau of Labor to question where the truth lay. No quick answer was found. The bureau sent a team to Detroit to discover if new equipment on 1966 models was the reason for price adjustments that could be rated as higher or lower than the prices for the 1965 cars.

Keeping the public's trust in both the national and the international landscapes was of colossal importance concerning the control of the automobile marketplace. The racing sport influenced the industry helping the average consumer dream of driving sportier and faster cars. The public demand was high; however, the political 'watchdogs' worked diligently to ensure these large conglomerates treated customers fairly, and that competition in manufacturing was competitive.

In an analytical article, the *Wall Street Journal* called it "sleight of hand" and awarded high marks in public relations to General Motors and Ford. According to the journal analyst, all automobile prices were higher, and the question was how skillfully the increases were covered up, and whether the labor statistics team, measuring safety devices and improved performance with their slide rules, would support this. This was important since their finding would enter the cost-of-living index. A lot turns on the index, including the wages of workers. The tizzy over prices dramatically illustrated how the auto industry dominated the American economy and how the motor car dominated the American way of life. One person in particular capitalized on the fluctuation of automobile fodder and actual costs in the mid-60s; that person was Bill Donoho.

In the BLS index, auto expenditures were 13% of all family costs and increased from 11.5% of all families' expenditures for the motor car in one form or another. In rural non-farm areas, it is 82%. The "sleight-of-hand" also illustrated how much more refined the industry had become. An anti-monopoly investigation into auto prices developed that in 1956, Ford announced an average increase of 2.9% for the 1957 models. Two weeks later, General Motors came along and reported Chevrolet prices were up 6.0%. A cynical witness at the hearings was Walter Reuther, head of the United Auto Workers Union, who said, "Now Ford was supposed to have established their prices based on cost figures. But what happened? As soon as General Motors announced higher prices, Ford revised their prices in line with GM. This was the first time in the history of a free enterprise economy where a company sets the price of their products to be competitive."

21. More Racing/Out of Prison

"Huntsville Speedway had attracted to that point and would, in the future, have a veritable "Who's Who" in racing in various categories of cars. Along with Petty, Jarrett, Weatherly, and the Bakers, Dale Earnhardt raced there, as did Davey, Bobby and Donnie Allison, Rusty Wallace, Mark Martin, and Neil Bonnett."

— Mark McCarter

The Huntsville Speedway was rated one of the finest quarter-mile asphalt tracks in the nation. It was sold to Bill Donoho and Bennie Goodman. However, there was some scuttlebutt within the industry about whether Donoho and Goodman purchased or leased the track. This track was built by Ashburn and Gray, Alabama road contractors, and cost $130,000 when it was constructed in 1964. Goodman and Donoho kept the actual cost under wraps however, as it was rumored to be just under the $100,000 figure. Gene Cato of Nashville, who had served as an official at the Fairgrounds Speedway, moved his family to Huntsville to serve as a full-time manager. The first program under Cato's direction ran on Thursday nights during the Spring and Summer until after Labor Day. Figure Eight Racing took place on Saturday nights. The first of these cards was held in early May 1967.

****

On December 28, 1968, Bill Donoho was released from the Federal Prison Camp at

Montgomery, Alabama, after serving approximately one-third of a 15-month sentence. Under federal regulations, a federal prisoner usually becomes eligible for parole after they have done a third of their time. Donoho entered the Federal Prison at Montgomery to begin serving his sentence after being convicted of tax evasion on July 1st. Donoho had been involved with the racing industry for approximately 15 years. After returning home, he went vacationing with his wife and son. He took some time to gather his game plan for promoting the Fairgrounds Speedway and other business interests.

As a businessman, my Great-Uncle Bill was brilliant. He knew how to assess a situation quickly, and had extensive knowledge of the economic market. Taking this time to strategize was his way of ensuring the rest of his life was as uneventful as possible while still being prosperous. Evidence of his intellect included an insistence that the Fairgrounds Speedway use top fuel and equipment for their drivers. He had placed the filling station in the in-field. This filling station serviced the high-powered cars with the same racing fuel used at Daytona and other superspeedways. Pure Oil Company supplied the mixture, containing additives that prevented the gasoline from boiling and creating a vapor lock that clogged the fuel line. The price of 50 cents a gallon was reasonable because of the high cost of the 1140 Octane Blend and special handling to get it to the tracks from the refinery. The addition of the filling station proved to be one of the Speedway's most profitable endeavors. Customers came from dragstrips and oval tracks up to 200 miles away for this gasoline.

****

Richard Petty was the 1969 sensation of Fairgrounds Speedway, but in the early days of the track, that honor belonged to Rex White, who gained the pole position for the first five races. Richard Petty's fifth-place finish in the Medal of Honor Firecracker 400 made him the highest major Speedway money winner in NASCAR'S 20-year history. Petty had won $324,405. Fred Lorenzen, who prosperously retired from racing, was second in major speedway winnings of $321,455, and David Pearson was third with $271,550. Petty also held the record for career money winnings with $640,859. To the average fan, racing cars for a living was what pipe dreams were made of, even when the smoke from the friction of rubber on asphalt dissipated into the air. These men and their winnings and actions enticed many others to get involved in racing.

Good racing doesn't occur without good mechanics, according to Harry Hyde. After 21 years of building and backing modifieds, sprints, and a few stockcars on USAC, ARCA, and independent tracks in the North and Midwest, Harry Hyde crossed the Mason-Dixon Line in 1966 to break into the NASCAR Grand National competition. The enthusiastic Louisville, Kentucky, native worked the K & K Insurance Dodge Team leader—a free entity until Dodge signed it at the beginning of the 1968 season. Hyde's cars were operated by various drivers, including Gordon Johncock and Earl Balmer, who entered nine races in 1966 but finished only one. In 1967 the situation improved for Hyde. He ran one car with Bobby Isaac and one car with Charlie Glotzbach as driver. The team consistently finished in the top ten significant events, including a second and fourth in the National 500 of Charlotte. Bobby Isaac bagged three victories and was runner-up to David Pearson in the Grand National point standings and won $44,530. Harry Hyde was finally getting his due recognition! Although still seeking a significant superspeedway win, Bobby Isaac and Harry Hyde proved practically invincible on NASCAR's short tracks, with Bobby collecting eight wins to lead all Grand National drivers in that category. Insiders said it was a matter of time until the pair won big. Something of an efficiency expert, Hyde believed that big-time racing can and must be approached scientifically and systematically.

22. The Speedway Family

"Mr. Goodman gave me the option to buy or sell and I believed enough in the future of racing to stay with it. I've been a part of it since the first boom and I feel it's one of America's favorite sports. I want to be a part of bringing the best races possible to the people of this area now and in the years to come."
— William "Bill" Donoho Sr.

Speaking of the future of racing locally, Bill Donoho, Sr. wanted it known that other people were involved in the purchase from Goodman. Donoho's wife, Mildred, would continue as one of the Speedways Vice-Presidents. His son, Jim, a student at the University of Tennessee, worked at the track during the summer. Bill Donoho named Bryan E. Burgess as the Vice-President of Nashville's Fairgrounds Speedway. Besides being a Vice President, Mr. Burgess was also a co-owner. The Speedway was fortunate to obtain a man of his caliber. Donoho stressed that the new structure within ownership would not cause any disruption in the scheduling of races. The new ownership structure brought in bigger and better attractions than ever before. Bill Donoho spent several days at Daytona Beach, Florida, developing the plans with NASCAR Executive Director Lin Kuchler and creating a new division. The new division would give local drivers a better opportunity to be competitive for national "Point of Honors."

Bill France, Assistant President of NASCAR, along with Bill Donoho and Bryan Burgess, developed plans to expand the Fairgrounds Speedway. The track was expanded from a half-mile to five-eigths-mile in 1970. The new track was 35 degrees in the turns and 12 degrees down the straightaways. Sixty percent of the track was in the turns and 40% in the straight. The racing groove that should enable cars to average well over 100 miles per hour was 30 feet wide, with another 10-foot groove for slower cars, plus a 10-foot-wide apron at the bottom of the track.

The existing half-mile track, constructed in 1958, was banked 23 degrees in the turns with flat straightaways. The track has always been one of the fastest on the NASCAR circuit, with speeds reaching more than 90 MPH. The new track and the elevation transition straightaway created concern about how many rows of seats would be lost. Each seat meant a ticket sold. Selling tickets was big business. An engineering firm from Warren Brother's Construction Company was hired to assess the situation. Some of the things that changed included: A new tunnel to allow entrance into the pits, which would be 12 feet wide, 16 feet high, and built with drainage, traffic lights, lighting, and gates; a 12-foot wide and 12-inch-deep sand pit was constructed between the track and the inside guard wall to provide a braking area and to reduce damage to cars spinning off the track; the existing lighting system was doubled; the current pit area was remodeled for the Hobby cars; and a new pit area was constructed concurrently with a new covered grandstand and a seating capacity of 18,500. The new grandstand cost more than half a million dollars. Cost of the track improvements was

$300,000. Construction on the grandstand and the racetrack began in early October 1969, and was up and ready for the 1970 racing season.

Nashville's Fairgrounds Speedway was chosen to host eight National Championship Races. Prize for the first sanctioned 100-lap (50-mile) race in the nation was $6,455. Excitement soared throughout the southeast and the racing sports world.

The success of the first 100-Lap race at the track made all its 100-Lap races Nationally sanctioned. The race brought a field of 42 cars to this high-banked track. It included National Point Leader Red Farmer from Hueytown, Alabama, and Bob Burcham from Chattanooga, Tennessee. Extra emphasis was put on points by NASCAR. The races drew top drivers from all over the country. Other 100-Lap races were held, including the Annual Jimmy Sawyer 100 and the Jim Reed 100. All these races paid 300 National Points. The Southern 300, the season's last race, held a purse of $15,000 plus 900 National Points.

The competition was exceptional. Joe Mangum had dominated Tuesday night late model unique auto racing at Fairgrounds Speedway by winning ten feature races. There were seven different winners in the Saturday night late model sportsman races. However, only Bob Burcham, with three wins, and Dave Sisco, with two, entered the victory circle more than once in the Saturday half-mile racetrack tests. Other winners besides Mangrum in the late model specials were Don Hobbs, John Rochelle, and Gen Ivey. Other late model sportsman victors were Flookie Buford, P. B.

Crowell, Jack Marlin, Gene Payne, and Gary Cook. Fast Saturday Qualifiers in the time trials were Ben Pruitt at 21.29 seconds, Jimmy Griggs at 21.22 seconds, among others.

23. Still Bending Rules

"I have ways of making money that you know nothing of."

– John D. Rockefeller

Bill Donoho was a genius for making money and finagling economic contracts that benefited himself and his family. The poverty he experienced as a young child led him to always be forward-thinking. He negotiated with the city of Nashville contracts that always served his needs and financial protections.

In 1965, Donoho moved to gain control of all food and drink concessions at the State Fairgrounds. This was evident when the Metro Council discovered that the concessions for the Nashville Fairgrounds Speedway were negotiated without using the bidding process. Five years later, Donoho still had the concessions for all but the week of the Tennessee State Fair. He also had control of all events staged at the Fairgrounds facilities.

Ambition to greatness pushed Donoho to use several tactics to control opportunities to continue bringing in the cash. Important steps by Bill Donoho in gaining the concession rights on the city-owned property included: the establishment of a corporation that once channeled 50% of all profits on wrestling concessions in the Fairgrounds Coliseum to a son of the former secretary-manager of the Fairgrounds, the late Clifford Andrews. These operations raised an estimated annual $12,000 each year since 1968, with no authority in writing. How he realized his dream to control the lucrative business, with the aid of Fairgrounds officials, is a study of how a man with influence enriched his fortune.

Bill Donoho was gifted at shuffling and maneuvering the legal means for developing contracts and creating financial windfalls for himself and others. Donoho also negotiated an agreement with the Metro Fair Board in 1969 which did not allow bids for handling concessions for events in the Fairgrounds buildings, except for wrestling. In the late 1960s, the Metro Fair Board operated without much oversite. The Fair Board neglected to keep proper minutes of their meetings, opening the door for some to question the legitimacy of Donoho's dealings with the city.

Ted Vaughan became manager when Andrews died in early 1968. "It was a bad situation for Mr. Andrews to have his son in a position to profit off the fairground operations benefitting financially with no accountability," Glenn Ferguson complained. "And it is equally bad business that Mr. Vaughan and his good friend Mr. Donoho are making money today off fairground purchases. Metro Council needed to do something about the situation. It seems obvious that the city administration and the Fair Board did not intend to correct it. Hence, the taxpayers only have recourse through the Metro Council." Fair Board Chairman John U. Wilson recently stated that neither he nor any other board members knew about the deal involving Andrews' son, and would not have permitted it if they had known. Wilson added that he had discussed the situation with Mr. Vaughan and assured the board nothing like the Andrews matter would happen again.

John U. Wilson, Fair Board Member was openly angered and flustered by the fairgrounds' situation. When the *Nashville Tennessean* asked John U. Wilson if he had a comment on the Vaughan-Donoho partnership, Wilson said, "Print whatever you damn well please, and don't call me again about nothing." Mr. Vaughan, when asked about his financial interest in the Fairground and purchases that he had made for the Fair Board from the firm, said he didn't think the situation was a conflict of interest. "Shannon Printing Company had always gotten the business before I was the manager." He added. "So, I just continued it. They [Shannon] already had all the printing plates on things we needed and regularly used." Vaughan explained that he purchased admission tickets and passes from Shannon and their prices "were as cheap as anybody's."

Donoho, when contacted, said he had previously owned a printing firm which he merged with Shannon Printing. The President of Shannon Printing was Shannon Colvett. Donoho felt strongly angered and stated dramatically that nothing was wrong with his wife and him owning a business. Again, Donoho felt the Metro Council discriminating against him, publicly questioning his business interests and, more importantly, his character.

Donoho formerly owned half interest in Job Printers, Inc.; however, he bought out his partner's interest in 1968. A few months later, when Vaughan became fairgrounds manager, Donoho merged his firm with Shannon Printing

Company. The firm had been at 37 Cleveland Street, Nashville. Ted Vaughan owned an interest in the printing company before he was hired as manager of the Fairgrounds Speedway.

Fairgrounds officials provided Donoho everything from free water for the Speedways to workhouse prisoners to clean up the racetrack. The Fairgrounds Speedway obtained a license to sell alcoholic beverages, mostly beer. More recently, the Fair Board arranged for Donoho to profit from beer being sold at Fairgrounds Coliseum on nights when wrestling matches were staged. In addition, Vaughan and the Fair Board had "pulled strings" for Donoho. In January 1969, Fair Board Chairman John U. Wilson signed an agreement extending Donoho's lease of the Speedways property until 1982, even though a professional study had been conducted that recommended against such action. The previous May, Vaughan signed a contract with Donoho, giving the ex-convict and former assistant police chief exclusive rights to food and drink concessions at nearly all events in the fairground's buildings. Donoho has been paying $100 a month to the Fair Board for this privilege. Mr. Wilson's attitude toward Donoho had softened as it was noted that Wilson and Vaughan signed the agreements with Donoho. However, no actions authorizing such deals were mentioned in the Fair Board's minutes. Nor are the contracts on file with the Metro clerk as the law requires. Nor were the agreements prepared and approved—as required by law—by the Metro Law Directors. Tempers flared over supposed unethical actions and lack of effort by the Fair Board to create a stronger oversite regarding all the Donoho Enterprises with the city of Nashville.

"It has been difficult to understand why Mr. Vaughan and the Fair Board were so eager to please Mr. Donoho," Metro Trustee Glenn Ferguson exclaimed. "But now it is a little clearer. Mr. Vaughan would not want to risk offending his business partner."

In 1963, Ted Vaughan worked for the Metro Board of (Tax) Equalization. Still, he resigned to prevent a conflict of interest due to the law ordinance that said Metro Boards and Commissions members could not do business with Metro. However, that ordinance does not apply to the Fair Board. Ferguson said he considered it "extremely bad practice for the head of a Metro Agency to be making purchases for his agency from a firm in which he has a financial interest." The trustee added, "It is operations like these that cause waste in government and cause the cost of local government to continue to increase." Before going to the fairgrounds, Vaughan was also a principal owner of Stoddard Office Supply Company, which sold Metro an estimated $125,000 worth of office equipment and supplies from 1963 to 1967.

Other concerns and conversations between Fairgrounds secretary-manager Ted Vaughan, Bill Donoho, and the Metro Fair Board included that Vaughan had solely relied on a 1966 entry in the board's minutes to justify giving a concessions contract to Donoho's Fast Service Company. However, the minutes recorded an agreement with Berlo Vending Company, a Miami firm.

Vaughan did acknowledge taking legal rights to the wrestling concession out of the contract that the Fair Board had with promoter Nick Gulas—without informing Nick Gulas of the action, which created more confusion for the Fair Board. And the concessions contract negotiated earlier in 1969 between Donoho and the Fair Board was not submitted to the Fair Board.

In 1969, an angry Metro Trustee, Glenn Ferguson, threatened to file a citizen's lawsuit to break Nashville Speedways' lease with the Metro Fair Board on the property at the State Fairgrounds. Ferguson stated that he might also seek to have the courts declare null and void a contract that fairgrounds manager Ted Vaughan gave to Bill Donoho to handle most food and drink concessions.

Donoho refused to comment on Trustee Ferguson's statements. John U. Wilson, chairman of the Fair Board, signed an agreement with Donoho in January which extended the Speedways' lease until 1987. In May, Mr. Vaughan signed a contract giving Donoho exclusive rights to the concession in fairgrounds buildings. Donoho paid $100 a month for concessions. Ferguson said that he was hopeful a lawsuit would not be necessary since Wilson asked the Metro Legal Department to examine the lease-extension agreement and the concessions contract. Wilson made the following request to the legal department: "It is my opinion," Ferguson said, "that both agreements with Mr. Donoho should be declared null and void because they were not entered into lawfully." The Trustee explained that there was no mention in the Fair Board's minutes of the lease extension or the concessions contract. Nor were the legal documents on file with the Metro clerk.

The concession contract was created without bids. Trustee Glenn Ferguson's concern was that neither document was prepared or approved beforehand by the Metro Legal Department, which was required by the Metro Charter. For this reason, Ferguson pledged to ask that the courts declare both contracts null and void. Ferguson said he contested the concessions contract and the lease extension at the time "because the city was getting ready to spend more than $700,000 out of bond funds to build grandstands to be used almost exclusively by Mr. Donoho and Nashville Speedways. Only once during the year will the grandstands be used for other purposes, which was the week of the Tennessee State Fair. If the Metro government had extra money to spend for improvements for some "privileged individual," I am sure the taxpayers would rather it go to departments they see benefits from, such as public works, the police department, or the fire department."

Meanwhile, a skating rink manager complained that Fairgrounds Roller Rink, located in a building rented from the Fair Board at what he termed "an amazingly low price," seriously threatened his business. Gene Fowler, owner and operator of Roller Drome-Skating Rink, 523 Thompson Lane, said, "$600 or 10% of gross receipts were paid monthly by Fairgrounds Roller Rink, which was less than one-third the rent he pays. He stated that he paid about $2,000 per month rent." Fowler said, "It appears like the city is putting our competition in business," explaining he felt the Metro Fair Board should have publicized that fairgrounds building were for rent so that others could have opportunities, such as Mr. Armstrong and Mr. Forrest Prince. He added that the location was excellent because everyone knows where [and could easily find] the fairgrounds. "If we had known the building was up for rent, we would have asked to rent it." In response, W. L. Armstrong, co-owner of Fairgrounds Roller Rink with Metro Councilman Forrest Prince, asked Fair Board Officials about renting the Fairgrounds exhibit building to have roller skating. "Most fairgrounds venues have a skating rink," Armstrong said. "I was amazed the Nashville Fairgrounds didn't have one here, so I asked about renting the building. It was approved."

24. More Shady Dealing

"The unforgivable political sin is vanity, the killer diet is sour grapes."
                                        – Neil Kinnock

Sleight-of-hand corruption continued to follow Bill Donoho through the 1970s. The newspaper reported Nashville Speedways owner Bill Donoho Sr told Metro Council's Executive Committee he did not think the Metro Fair Board had given him any favors. Donoho added that he had not expected in 1965 to receive anything special in return for giving the then fairgrounds manager's son 50% of a lucrative concessions business. The Speedways President testified at length about his business association with George Grady Andrews, son of the late Clifford Andrews, but denied anything improper in the relationship. Clifford Andrews was Fairground's manager from 1961 until he died in 1968. Ted Vaughan succeeded Andrews as Fairgrounds Manager. Members of the executive committee questioned Donoho at length about All Sports Inc., a corporation that Donoho formed to manage food and drink concessions at the Fairgrounds Coliseum on nights when wrestling was held. Donoho was given the concession rights by wrestling promoters – Nick Gulas and Roy Welch – who staged the wrestling matches in the Coliseum, which they rented from the Metro Fair Board.

Bennie Goodman, a former partner of Donoho's in All Sports, Inc. and Nashville Speedways, had said previously he and Donoho cut George Grady Andrews in on the concessions business "to get favors from his father." Under close questioning by Metro Councilman James Warren, Donoho acknowledged giving George Grady half of All Sports' Inc. profits, but denied it was done to get favors from the elder Andrews. "I don't think I've ever gotten any favors," Donoho added. "What did it cost George Grady Andrews to get involved in All Sports?" Donoho said, "The contract says $1 and 'other valuable considerations.'" Metro Councilman Warren continued. "What were the other 'valuable considerations?' Just that...a dollar?" Why did you go to George Grady Andrews in the first place?" Donoho stated, "Well, I had just heard he wanted to be in this business." Metro Councilman pressed hard on Donoho, questioning what Mr. Andrews did in return for the profits he earned. "It appeared he got something like $4,000 a year." "He came out there [to the fairgrounds] a few times. He attended all the meetings," Donoho stated. Frustrated, Warren continued his inquisition. "Mr. Andrews was just a figurehead in this corporation. Why was Andrews a part of the firm? Did you go to Mr. Clifford Andrews and ask for any special favors?" Donoho firmly answered that he did not. Warren stated, patronizingly, that it was difficult for him to understand why Donoho would give George Grady Andrews $4,000 annually without expecting anything in return. "I wouldn't give that kind of money away without expecting something in return, and it's tough for me to understand why, as smart of a businessman as you are, why you would give it away." Donoho replied that he had no special reason for doing it. "Didn't you expect something out of George Grady Andrews," Warren asked. "I expected some work out of him," Donoho replied. "I got some, but not much." Warren then told the executive committee he was "disappointed at Mr. Donoho's answers." George Grady Andrews had previously told newsmen that he got into All Sports Inc. at his father's suggestion, and that he did not do any work for the money he received except to attend a few meetings. Mr. Andrews added that as soon as his father died, it seemed Mr. Donoho didn't need him anymore, and he was forced out. Donoho denied forcing Mr. Andrews out after the elder Andrews died. "Still, this all seemed strange to me," Warren complained. It has been alleged that Donoho had received numerous partialities from the Metro Fair Board, including 1) the right to handle food and drink concessions for most events held in the fairground, 2) The right to realize a profit from the sale of beer in the Fairgrounds Coliseum on nights that wrestling matches were staged, 3) A favorable lease of fairgrounds property to be used for operating the Speedways as an auto racetrack, and 4) Free water and use of workhouse prisoners to clean up after the races. Donoho acknowledged he got the unrestricted use of workhouse prisoners, but he denied he got free water.

Frank Ritter, a reporter for The *Nashville Tennessean*, testified before the Executive Committee regarding concerns he raised about the Speedway's and Fairground's operations in several newspaper articles. Glenn Ferguson,

Metro Trustee, testified about the tax assessment on the Speedways and told the council committee, "Mr. Donoho and Mr. Vaughan moved in wanting control of every aspect of the fairgrounds." Ferguson said he had told the Executive Committee, that he had been openly critical of the tax assessment on Nashville Speedways, labeling it much too low. "As Nashville's tax collector, people complain all the time about how hard it is for them to pay their taxes. That is why I expressed frustration at what I feel is a bad situation with the Fairgrounds."

The council's executive committee launched a probe of the fairgrounds and the Speedways. No action was taken at the meeting except the passage of a resolution asking that Mayor Beverly Briley submit recommendations on what he thought should be done to tighten operations at the fairgrounds. Several councilmen suggested the Metro Fair Board be brought under Metro's purchasing ordinance so the city administration could more closely guard its operation. The executive committee expected to recommend this once its probe was formally completed. Others expected to be called by the committee include George Grady Andrews, Bennie Goodman, and Mark Parrish. Both Goodman and Parrish declined to appear before the committee, stating that they would only agree to testify under oath and that everyone else that was questioned was also questioned under oath.

25. Dirty Driving

"I am often thought of as being remarkably bright, and yet my brains, more often than not, are busily devising new and interesting ways of bringing my enemies to sudden, gagging, writhing, agonizing death."
— *Alan Bradley, The Weed That Strings the Hangman's Bag*

During the days of Bob Riker, some fans swear they saw him go the wrong way on the track to gain vengeance on another driver who had rubbed him the wrong way. It had been many years since Riker, but the drivers had themselves a new villain in Flookie Booth Buford. Participants on the five-eighths-mile oval at Fairgrounds Speedway discussed putting a bounty on Buford's head. The President of the track, Bill Donoho, talked the drivers out of this and instead into filing a formal protest with NASCAR against Flookie Buford. A turbulent scene occurred after a Sunday race when Flookie Buford and Don Anthony collided in the three-fourths turn. However, Anthony was in the lead, and Flookie Buford pushed forward to the front for the victory. There was talk of "getting" Flookie now and going to Donoho later. Ken Wiser, co-owner of Don Anthony's car, told how owners had discussed putting up $340 to the man who'd put Flookie Buford out, and then pay for the assassin to get his car fixed. Reaching out with complaints had been Ken Wiser, Don Anthony, P. B. Crowell, Charlie Binkley, Bill Morton, and James Hamm, according to the track co-owner Donoho. Even Ken Wiser thought putting a bounty on Buford was too radical, and after talking to Donoho, they agreed to reach out to NASCAR officials. In a letter to Mr. Lee, Cultural Executive Vice President of NASCAR, Ken Wiser charged that during this season, Buford had caused or wrecked Bob Burcham, Don Anthony, Charles Binkley, P. B. Crowell, and Darrell Waltrip; moreover, Ken Wiser charged that during the 1970 season, Buford wrecked Bunkie Blackburn, Dave Sisco, and George Bonds. Ken Wiser's letter was a statement that he was behind Donoho for events occurring the past Saturday night, which saw him lead up and then get brought back on the gas and knock Don Anthony into the wall in turn three. Don Anthony said Flookie Buford never gave up and ran him into the wall. Ken Wiser's letter said Flookie Buford drove straight into the left door and left tire marks for everyone to see.

Buford put fear in all the drivers that ran with him. Most drivers believe it was deliberate since Flookie Buford was on this track every time he pulled this stunt. Most cars can't get close enough to get tied in with them. So, he banks off and goes around without problems with his car. Still, drivers kept complaining, and criticisms had mushroomed. Donoho sent a letter of his own pointing out that he would like to solve his problems. The letter continued protesting Buford, stating that whoever was next to Buford and lining up for the featured event dreads the start of the race. Mentioning the bounty talk, Donoho said he told drivers, car owners, and mechanics that it better not happen. Any person's involvement in such vengeance would be barred for life. Preventing accidents at high speeds was the main concern, said Donoho, who recommended that NASCAR impose a rule strictly for the Fairgrounds Speedways whereby any car causing the lead car to spin or be knocked into the wall must go to the rear. The recommendation also stated that many felt that Flookie Buford was driving a little over his head, and that NASCAR should suspend him for 30 days. Donoho's last recommendation was that Flookie Buford be put on 30-day probation once the suspension was lifted. Given the facts, except perhaps the version of Flookie Buford, Mr. Kuchler could decide exactly how anybody could prove one man deliberately hit another. They couldn't "eye-prove" that Riker gradually turned in the wrong direction purposefully to cause wrccks, and I don't remember Bob owning up to it. Bob Riker was probably grinning somewhere, and might even consider returning to the races.

26. Racetrack Woes

"There is only one boss. The customer. And he can fire everybody in the company from the chairman on down, simply by spending his money somewhere else."
– Sam Walton

The contract for food and drink concession at the State Fairgrounds, which had never been opened on a competitive basis, was awarded to a new competitor, Nashville businessperson William R. "Red" Jordan. Jordan, manager of Blevins Popcorn Company in Nashville and owner of Red and White Liquor Store, was the only person to enter a bid for the concessions. When bids were opened, Ted Vaughan, Fairgrounds Manager, explained. "One of the problems with getting people to bid," Vaughan said, "was that we did not know exactly what activities would occur at the Fairgrounds. They didn't know exactly how much they would have to work on the thing." The contract stipulated that Jordan should pay Metro 22% of his gross earnings. Vaughan shared that the previous agreement with Fast Service Company allowed owner Bill Donoho to pay the city $100 monthly or 5% of gross earnings, depending on which was more significant. "We have agreed that the new contract offers a fair price." Jordan began handling the concessions immediately at the wrestling matches in Fairgrounds Coliseum. Vaughan added, "We are glad to see this thing open on a competitive basis." During a probe into fairground operations, Vaughan and Metro

Fair Board Chairman John U. Wilson promised
Metro Council's Executive Committee that the
concessions contract would be open for bids
when Donoho's contract expired on July 1. The
first contract for the Fairgrounds concession
was June 30, 1965, to Gulas-Welch Wrestling
Enterprises. Donoho, the principal owner of
Nashville Speedways Inc., took over the
concession on May 1, 1969, after he formed the
Fast Service Company.

Bill Donoho, President of Fairground
Speedways, released statistics refuting criticism
of the new five-eighth mile track. Drivers and
racing officials had leveled brutal blasts at the
track for the high attrition rates in longer races.
Donoho said the criticism was unjustified and it
threatened the future of racing here. Specifically
referring to an article in the *Southern
Motorsports Journal*, Donoho labeled
statements untrue by NASCAR Vice-President
Lin Kuchler, saying that the track was too fast
for Sportsman cars and that the equipment
could not stand up under such conditions in a
long race. "True, the attrition rate was very high
in the Flameless 300, in which only nine cars
were running at the end," said Donoho. "But this
happens at all tracks from time to time."
Donoho noted that tracks at Darlington, S.C.,
Richmond, VA., Ona, W. Va., and Maryville had
only 11 or 12 cars running at the end of long
races. "These were all Grand National Races,"
Donoho said. Donoho said statements such as
Kuchler's would cause drivers to be reluctant
about racing at the Fairgrounds Speedway, and
he pointed to an incident that seemed to
substantiate his fears.

Red Farmer, late model Sportsman National Champion, told track publicity director Joe Carver of the rumors he'd heard about the track. "From what I've heard," said Farmer, somewhat jokingly, "you almost need a tank to run up there." A great deal of controversy about the new track, which had some of the world's steepest banks at 35 degrees, involved undue wear on the chassis and tires. A series of tire tests with different compounds solved the latter problem. Donoho maintains that only two cars in the Flameless 300 were forced to leave because of abnormal situations. According to Carver, the attrition rate in 300-lap races had not increased from that on the half-mile track. Carver's figures showed that 7 and 11 had been running at the end of the 300-lap races on the old track in the past seven years. "Most of the top drivers said they only had to turn their engines 6500 to 6800 RPM on the new track," said Donoho. "That was much less than the 7200 to 7400 RPM that had to be turned on the half-mile track."

27. Getting a Little Help

"It was like a professional playing with amateurs."

– Benny Parsons

Is there any sentiment in racing? "Yes, there's a great deal of it," said Benny Parsons. Parsons, who won $52,325 as a Grand National driver in 1970, made his fifth season appearance in the Music City Grand Guitar 100-lap Sportsman's Division here. He did it to repay a debt he felt he owed Fairgrounds Speedways and Bill Donoho. "When I was down, he picked me up, and if I can help him draw people to his track, I'll be there whenever it's humanly possible."

It is not unique, but it is unusual, for Grand National drivers to drop down to the Sportsman's Division. Benny Parsons had not done it for three or four years until he made the first five appearances in Nashville in July 1971. Benny's unusual situation arose when the owner of his Grand National car, L. G. Dewitt, suffered a severe injury in a street accident earlier in the year. L. G. Dewitt decided to leave racing, and Benny Parsons was out of a job. "I had a choice of going back to Detroit, where my father and I own a taxicab company, or trying to find another way to race in the South. I like racing and living in the South, so I decided to travel to Daytona and see what I could do. Mr. Donoho asked me to visit Nashville for a Sportsman's race. He said he would pay my expenses and provide me with a good car. What did I have to lose? I did not make much money in that first race, finishing seventh, but the next time I won. I decided that if Mr. Donoho would do that for me, maybe some other owner would too. I called Birmingham, and they were willing. Bobby Allison runs in the Sportsman's division all the time, as well as in Grand National races, but this is the first time for me since 1967." Parsons won $6,400 at Riverside in January, driving the Dewitt car. Still, he didn't enjoy another big payoff until he finished third in Atlanta for a $6,200 purse.

He made it back in the Grand National business—owner of his cars, two of them. "I bought a 1969 Ford from Mr. Dewitt," Benny Parsons stated. "After the Atlanta race, he had a few bucks, so he bought his other car, a 1971 model, which was used too, but most of us just do it because we like it. There's no good answer to what makes a racecar driver come back for more, but I guess he gets addicted, just like a man on dope, whiskey, or smoking. I enjoy it, and that's more important than money."

28. Chairman of the Board

Who leaves the real legacy?

"If your actions create a legacy that inspires others to dream more, learn more, do more and become more, then, you are an excellent leader."

– Dolly Parton

Who's the best driver to ever perform at the Fairgrounds Speedway? A panel of veterans who observed and researched races held there over the past few years came up with answers to that question recently, and then they broke it down. Coo Coo Marlin, of Columbia, Tennessee, is the best local sportsman-modified driver. The best Grand National driver is Richard Petty of Randleman, North Carolina. The best driver of any kind of car in the world was A. J. Foyt. The selection included Tom Powell of The *Nashville Tennessean* and Bill Donoho, credited with fathering racing in Nashville in 1946, and track publicist Joe Carver. Marlin was a three times local Sportsman-Modified champion (1963) and still held the record for the most career wins with 36. Petty raced in every Grand National event at the Speedways and won top money six times. A. J. Foyt won his "best in the world" label due to successes at Indianapolis, where he won three times in NASCAR stocks and on European road races.

Bill Donoho, Chairman of the Board of Nashville Speedways, Inc., spearheaded stock car racing in Nashville from its beginning and directed it to become Nashville's No. 1 Sport in 1971. In 1970, Bill Donoho realized a long-time dream by opening the world's fastest five-eighths mile track with the steepest banks (35 degrees) of any NASCAR nationwide track. Owners and promoters for every track on the NASCAR circuit came to Nashville to see the layout that caused quite a commotion in racing circles. William "Bill" Donoho said that the new oval served as a model for other tracks around the Southeast.

Bill Donoho started promoting races at the Legion Bowls on Cowan Avenue in 1949. In 1958, he was the driving force behind establishing the country's most successful short-track operation when racing was moved to its present location on the Fairgrounds. Many a checkered flag had been dropped since 1949, and each year the sport's popularity mushroomed. Bill Donoho's Speedway was one more "plus" in the "plus city."

Since the early 1890s, the area near Nolensville Road, now occupied by Fairgrounds Speedway, was built as Cumberland Park for horse racing. The original track was considered one of the finest in the area. As early as the State Fair of 1890, it was used for auto races. But even though parimutuel betting was outlawed and thoroughbred racing had left Tennessee by 1910, the site remained horse country. Horse Shows and harness races were held there for 50 years, but only once a year, during the State Fair, were automobiles permitted to race on the extensive dirt course. By 1957, auto racing had come into its own after it was started regularly, shortly after World War II. More comprehensive facilities for the weekly events were needed to accommodate the ever-increasing crowds. The Legion Bowl on Cowan Avenue was much too small. Speedways Promoter Bill Donoho set his sights on the Fairgrounds. When the horsemen who controlled the site said they didn't want to move, a controversy ensued. The differences were resolved in 1958.

The equestrians moved to a new training center in Brentwood. Donoho and the auto races officially got the Fairgrounds. Nashville Speedways, Inc. called for a new concept in automobile races by building two tracks in one. By utilizing the front straightaway, the facilities included a quarter-mile track and the high-banked, half-mile track. The first race on the new track was held in July 1958. It was a 200-lap NASCAR Grand National event. A crowd of 13,988 fans turned out to see the late Joe Weatherly take the checkered flag in the first of many spectacular Grand National events to follow this initial race. The years between 1958 and 1970 became a well-known success story for auto racing in Nashville. As the sport continued its phenomenal growth nationally, it became an exciting segment of the Nashville sports scene. Under Donoho's supervision, the sport attracted record attendance.

The old half-mile track, where drivers thrilled the crowds for a dozen years, was gone. It was replaced by the five-eighths mile track directed by Donoho under a contract agreement through 1987. As of 1971, the new oval was declared officially by NASCAR to be the fasted five-eighths stock car track in the world. LeeRoy

Yarborough held the NASCAR Grand National speed record at 119.668 miles per hour. He set the mark while qualifying for the Nashville 420. Local sportsman driver James Hamm set the Sportsman mark on May 14, 1971, at 121.228 miles per hour. Where will it end? Many racing experts believed 125 miles per hour was not out of reach. One thing was for sure, whether it was 119 mph or 125 mph, the cars combined with the fastest short track in the world provided spectators with a show unrivaled in Nashville for excitement. To a large segment of the Nashville sports-loving public, the Fairgrounds were the scene of a spectacle of noise and color that had become the city's Number 1 gate attraction.

29. Jimbo Donoho

"Great entrepreneurial DNA is comprised of leadership, technological vision, frugality, and the desire to succeed."

– Steve Blank

Jim Donoho, the 22-year-old son of Bill Donoho, stated publicly that he planned to make a million dollars by the time he turned 30. He owned a company that he assessed at $500,000. The ambitious young entrepreneur was the owner of American Furniture Leasing Inc., which was in the business of leasing furniture for houses, apartments, offices, and other institutions. Jim was an innovative man like his father, always following a vision. His company also made furniture, as well as refinished and upholstered furniture. The business employed 15 people. The younger Donoho started with a 6,800 sq. ft. building. However, within three years, he expanded to a 25,000 sq. ft. building and owned the five-story adjacent building. The company had a surging client base. Some customers included people like flight attendants who needed furniture for eight or nine months, and many couples who had just married. Jim created one of the first rent-to-own furniture businesses. If the client leased the furniture for 36 months, the client owned the furniture—a complete bedroom suite rented from $15 a month to $125. The quality was competitive. Jim even used leased furniture in his apartment. Jim Donoho was proud of his position within the company and grinned like a

132

Cheshire Cat. His office included an oversized, black vinyl plush chair. He said, "I'll lease anything anybody wants."

Jim began his furniture business with a partner, Martin Bublis, who was a couple of years older. His father was heard saying, "Who wants to lease furniture?" However, the elder Donoho didn't take long to recognize a good money-maker. American Furniture Leasing Inc. had contracts for up to five years. Jim and his managers had no issue contacting other furniture companies and inviting their customers to check out the new rent-to-own furniture. The business was booming. The company had $45,000 worth of models in apartment buildings for people to view. In June 1971, Young Jim Donoho bought out Bubis' share of the business.

Jim was also the track president at Fairgrounds Speedway, where his father, Bill Donoho was board chairman. Jim had been around the speedway all his life. He knew the business well and said, "My father began working with me early. He had me selling cigarettes out there when I was seven years old. The first night I came up fifty cents short, and he took it out of my pay. I was never short again." Through his teenage years, Jim worked at the racetrack in various jobs, including ticket sales and track announcer, after attending Bill Hudson School of Broadcasting. He was also president of one of the concessions companies at the fairgrounds. He participated in the races until his father asked him to stop.

"Dad asked me one day, 'How much do you owe us?' and I replied $250,000." The father asked his son if he could pay it off today. Jim said, "No," and he said, "Well, stop driving race cars," so Jim didn't drive race cars anymore. The elder Donoho could not take on the responsibility of allowing his son to possibly be injured as a racecar driver.

On weekends, Jim traveled around to out-of-state races. Jim attended the University of Tennessee in Knoxville for two years and majored in finance. While there, he was in business with his father in the Dinner Club of America, through which members held tickets for meals at reduced prices at various Knoxville restaurants. At 22, Jim attended the UT-Nashville campus. Jim was an avid golfer. He played in golf tournaments around the area and held several trophies. He had lettered in tennis for three years at Hillwood High School. Jim was not only athletic; he studied piano for 14 years and won second place in the state for his musical ability. "I often play the organ during the press parties at the fairgrounds. In Knoxville, I had a routine with jokes while playing the organ," he said.

In 1969, Jim took time to get married. "Beverly, my wife, worked five days a week at First American National Bank, went to art school two nights a week, and sold tickets at the racetrack two nights." Jim told her that if she was going to marry a Donoho, she'd have to work. There were no dead weights in the family. Beverly worked as hard and fast as the rest of the Donoho clan.

30. Blood Sport

*Wrestling Fans at the Fairgrounds Coliseum
Enjoy the Show*

*"It's a little like wrestling a gorilla. You don't
quit when you're tired- you quit when the
gorilla is tired."*
– Robert Strauss

The NWA, National Wrestling Alliance, was the
most dominant wrestling body throughout the
1950s, and wrestling promotions were under
their leadership. However, many felt that the
NWA refused to push new and innovative ideas
into the sport. As a result, many promoters
separated from the NWA. They found
opportunities to promote wrestling elsewhere,
eventually evolving into the American Wrestling
Association (AWA) during the 1960s. World
Wrestling Federation (WWF) and World
Heavyweight Championship wrestling followed.

The Nashville Fairgrounds Coliseum hosted
many events, from circus to classic car shows.
However, in 1965 wrestling promoters Nick
Gulas and Roy Welch brought the NWA–
National Wrestling Alliance–to the coliseum.
The crowds came to cheer on their favorite
wrestlers, drink beer, and snack on the
concessions under Bill Donoho's authority.
Many of Donoho's family members worked the
concessions two nights a week, making huge
profits. Over the next few years, the sport of
wrestling grew in Nashville. The enthusiastic
fans at the Fairgrounds Arena Coliseum had

plenty to cheer about in December 1971. The competition was fierce. A Nashville Amateur Boxing Association fighter won three out of five decisions with sluggers from Jackson, Tennessee. Larry Jackson of the Dickey Boarding House entry was the loser in the opening match. Still, he showed fine against Willie Johnson, weighing 148 pounds. Don Morgan was magnificent in the first round against Robert Clark, but he barely held his own in the final two sessions. The judging saw Richard Kuchinski and Dr. Sam Bernow awarded it to Don Morgan 53-38, while Jim Bow scored it against Don Morgan 61-59. Reaching back for a little extra, Arrington, a Marine who staged a strong finish to win his match on a split decision, Jim Donoho scored the fight for Robinson, 61-59, while his father, Bill Donoho had it 69-59 for Arrington and Bow. Kuchinski called it 60-69 with a nod to Arrington. Eddie Williams was extremely sharp initially, but almost ran out of steam by the time the final bell rang. Thursday's Program was a Ladies' Night, with all women escorted and admitted to the match for free. Wrestling became very popular in Nashville. In 1968, Nick Gulas and Roy Welch were labeled the "Promoters of the Year" at the Fairgrounds. Bill Donoho Sr. worked hard to be involved in large portions of every "pie" associated with the Fairgrounds.

31. Bigger Dreams

"Everything you want is out there waiting for you to ask. Everything you want also wants you. But you have to take action to get it."
— *Jules Renard*

Negotiations were underway on three possible sites for a proposed multimillion-dollar sports arena with ice hockey, basketball, wrestling, boxing, and concert facilities. Bill Donoho, an executive with the Fairgrounds Speedway and one of the financial backers of the proposed arena, said there are three sites within the city's interstate highway loop. Authorities of the Nashville Housing Authority confirmed that at least one of Donoho's sites was a 17-acre tract along South Street at 12th Avenue, South. That site was also of interest to the Metro Board of Hospitals as a possible site for a $20 million comprehensive Metro Health Center. This facility would allow the phasing out of the Nashville General Hospital and Bordeaux hospitals. Donoho stated he and other financial backers had guaranteed financing of $2 million. He said the proposed sports facility would cost less than $3 million. Architectural work on the 5,000-seat facility was already underway. Donoho had discussed his proposal with Nashville Housing Authority staff members and received strong support. Jack Herrington, NHA executive director, met Monday with Leslie Vantreace, Chairman of the Metro Hospital Board, and Dr. Phillip Neel Jr., Metro Hospital Director. Donoho was assisted in dealing with the NHA by Councilman Mansford Douglas III, representing those living South of Nashville. Douglas was chairman of the council's Hospitals, Health, and Welfare Committee. Douglas said he'd like to see the property used for recreational purposes and possible shopping services for area residents. The property that was discussed was presently zoned for residential use and would specifically allow the construction of a multi-family development. Many were excited about an arena because it was thought it could be a way to amend the urban renewal plan so that they would not build more high-density apartment units in the Edgehill area. Douglas had recently asked the NHA to amend the plan from residential zoning to a commercial zoning category to permit such a use.

Donoho confirmed that the arena was first discussed by Joe Carver, publicity man for the Speedway, during a meeting with citizens interested in bringing ice hockey to Nashville. Carver said that he was speaking on behalf of a group of businessmen interested in building a recreational arena. There would be plenty of parking space, and it would be about a three-minute drive from downtown.

32. Too Fast; Too Dangerous

"There is no such thing as bad publicity except your own obituary."
— *Brendan Behan*

The saying "Tell it like it is" fits NASCAR Grand National driver Bobby Isaac who drove for K & K Dodge. Isaac won the first race on the five-eighths-mile track at Fairgrounds Speedway in July 1970. He was also the first driver to criticize the high-banked super-fast track. Quoting Isaac, "This track (Nashville Fairways Speedway) is too fast and too dangerous!" as he was handed the five-foot trophy and a microphone. The words that Isaac hawked out that fiery day after the race to "ABC Wide World of Sports" cameras made Speedways President Bill Donoho raging mad. Bobby Isaac pledged never to return, regardless of the prize. Though Donoho didn't admit it, Isaac's horrific words that afternoon were the best thing the 1970 NASCAR Grand National Champion could have said. Since that first race, the stands were full almost every race night. Race fans throughout the South flocked to the racetrack to see the place where a man who holds the land speed record said it was too fast. The possibility of witnessing a significant crash while glowering over the anticipation of the disaster was the best publicity an industry like racing could get. Who could resist looking it right in the eye? Isaac also returned.

The previous year, the Catawba, North Carolina, performer started as the fourth fastest in the 420. He was out for the night before the first lap had been completed. He and Coo Coo Marlin got too close coming out of the second turn, and both crashed into the wall, ending the race for both. Bobby Isaac and Bill Donoho eventually resolved their differences. Isaac went into the record books for the 420 as a competitor who couldn't complete even one lap. Many drivers jokingly said that Donoho could put a curse on you if you didn't act right. Superstitions about Isaac's angry words and Donoho's fury were taken seriously.

Bobby Isaac joined the elite Grand National stars: Bobby Allison, Richard Petty, Cale Yarborough, Buddy Baker, Donnie Allison, Darrell Waltrip, Coo Coo Marlin, Benny Parsons, Lennie Pond, Vick Parsons, Dave Marcis, and Dave Sisco. Shortly after the Nashville 420, Bobby Isaac split with the K & K Insurance Dodge that Buddy Baker was driving. The dispute reportedly came when crew Chief Harry Hyde wanted Baker to drive a second car for K & K. So, Isaac propelled a Bud Moore Ford in the 420 at Nashville. He struggled to find victory in the Moore Ford. Still, he finished second to Richard Petty in Daytona 500, second to David Pearson in the Atlanta 500, and fourth at Richmond. He won over $30,000 in the seven races.

33. The Need to Conserve

"The Fairgrounds Speedway Recognized the Need to Conserve"

Toward the end of 1973, crude oil prices mandated by the (OPEC) Organization of Petroleum Exporting Countries, rose from $1.62 per barrel in January, to $3.15 in October, to $7.11 in January 1974. No price control system could address the rapid, steep rise in oil. The year 1974 was one of the worst annual inflation rates in the country's history. In the fourth quarter of 1974, the GNP declined at an annual rate of 5.8%, and unemployment was at a vertical high. This period of the 1970s was dubbed The Great Inflation. Political leaders supporting monetary policies that financed massive budget deficits were the cause. With inflation, automobile racing had to tighten its belt and exist on less fuel. Promoter Bill Donoho and his staff had to cut racing laps by 30%. The energy shortage made Racing Speedways everywhere get creative regarding cutbacks. NASCAR President Bill France called on all affiliated tracks to cut back 20-25%. Donoho and his staff went to work. They cut back 1,500-plus laps by eliminating Friday night racing and qualifying rounds for big Sportsman and Grand National events. By Col. Gil Smith's analysis, they saved 250 gallons of fuel from electricity alone. Donoho stated that he had purchased nearly 13,000 gallons of high-octane racing gasoline the previous year, and nearly 1,000 gallons were still in the tanks. Union 76 assured the Speedway executives that the track would have the racing fuel it needed for the year.

The track had other plans for conserving fuel. Saturday night racing started 30 minutes earlier to save electricity, and all programs were over by 10 o'clock. The lights were turned off three minutes after the race. The Fairgrounds Speedway also encouraged carpools. Cars that had at least six people received one ticket free. Some tracks eliminated non-counting yellow laps during a race by simply stopping the race to conserve fuel. For Nashville Speedways, clearing the track quicker cut down on yellow laps. Donoho expected the year to be a good year, with most of the fans traveling less than 50 miles to attend races. Donoho made sure the year was fuel-conscious, entertaining, and profitable.

There were some changes in the drivers to keep interest high. Darrell Waltrip drove R. C. Alexander's Ford. Flookie Buford drove the No. 88, James Francis' car piloted by James Hamm the previous year. Hamm moved to the Ellis Cook team, where Waltrip was the top driver in the 1973 year. Waltrip ran his Terminal Transport Mercury in the Sportsman Race at Daytona.

34. Chauvinist of the Year

"Hopefully, in the future, generational challenges will be measured by achievement, not gender."

– Safra A. Catz

On October 6, 1974, according to Mrs. Kathy Speakman, William J. "Bill" Donoho Sr. overwhelmingly won the "Nashville's Male Chauvinist of the Year" award because he banned women from doing anything at his racetrack except spending their money. Nashville's racing Czar refused to allow the young Alabama woman, a licensed NASCAR driver with her own race car, to serve as a member of her husband's pit crew. Donoho did not give a reason or explanation. When he was asked why he wouldn't let Mrs. Speakman participate, his answer was short and simple: "There is no reason. We do not allow women to race." Mrs. Kathy Speakman had been encouraged to enter races by an Alabama promoter who wanted to attract family audiences and improve the sport's image. Many were angry at this narrow-minded attitude. Mrs. Speakman was publicly embarrassed to be discriminated against. She told reporters she wasn't a troublemaker and had been racing all summer, with no complaints. For damage control, Donoho later told his audiences that their organization was close to 50-50 males and females. Reporters observed that Donoho didn't object to female fans buying tickets to his racetrack. Mrs. Speakman was encouraged to take legal action against the promoter, who leased his land from taxpayers under an advantageous arrangement. But she preferred to forget her bad experience with Donoho and compete on tracks where she could boost crowds for other promoters.

35. Jimbo's Biscuits

"You gotta risk it to get the biscuit."
--Jimmy Fallon

Jim Donoho, who wanted to make a million dollars before turning 30, used his entrepreneurial skills to create a new business called "Jimbo." Jim announced plans in January 1976 for a new twist in the fast-food industry. Jim Donoho planned an entire menu around the biscuit. The idea was founded by the parent company, Old Fashioned Food Inc., which said that the first Jimbo's Biscuit Barn opened in February 1976, and five more were added in December 1976. Jimbo's Biscuit Barn served ten items that could be eaten in or on biscuits, with three side dish options. Jim was the organizer, President, and sole stockholder of the parent company that furnished the real estate and supplies for operating Jimbo's Biscuit Barn, Inc. Along with the meal, coffee was sold for ten cents a cup. Jim's spirited attitude was noted, and he was quoted often as saying, "We will make money, even with coffee 10 cents a cup."

Like his father and namesake, Jim Donoho was an innovative, forward-thinking businessman whose sole goal was to make money. Donoho was among a faction of about 35 investors. His corporation was a closed corporation. A 10-man Board of Directors and a five-person Executive Committee were elected to manage the company. The restaurants had barn-type architecture, rough wood interior walls, rustic décor and furnishings, and barn-wood fronts.

While Jim Donoho's finance skills were successful and popular, his personal life took quite a hit. His marriage to the lovely Beverly Donoho ended in divorce. However, on July 6, 1976, Jim remarried a beautiful young lady named Rosalynn, daughter of Mr. and Mrs. William Clift, from Hartsville, Tennessee. Rosalynn was a registered nurse with the Tennessee Foundation for Medical Care.

36. Rain, Rain, Go Away

*"If you think of life as like a big pie, you can try
to hold the whole pie and kill yourself trying to
keep it, or you can slice it up and give some to
the people around you, and you still have
plenty left for yourself."*

– Jay Leno

*William "Bill" Donoho Wants Controlling
Interests in Every "Piece of the Nashville Pie"*

In April 1978, Councilman Charles French
suggested that Bill Donoho be considered for
managing the Municipal Auditorium. This
frustrated and caused scuttle among city
officials. The councilman noted that Donoho,
who operated the Nashville Fairgrounds
Speedway at the State Fairgrounds, had shown
ingenuity and success in his business endeavors.
However, John U. Wilson, Chairman of the
Board of Commissioners of the Fairgrounds,
challenged French's idea. Councilman French
urged the mayor–Richard Fulton, at the time–
and the Municipal Auditorium Commission to
consider putting the financially troubled
auditorium in the hands of an independent
contractor, such as Donoho. In a resolution to
the Commission, French stated, "Bill Donoho,
through his management and promotional
talents, turned an enterprise that was costly to
taxpayers of Nashville and Davidson County
into an enterprise that not only paid its way but
gave a significant return to the citizens of the
community." Wilson questioned the accuracy of
the statement that Donoho's actions resulted in

the financial success of the fairgrounds, but added he was not trying to discredit Donoho; he intended to point out that Donoho was just a "spoke in the wheel," not the whole machine. Wilson resented the illusion that Donoho did everything by himself without acknowledging the work of many others involved with the success of the Nashville Fairgrounds Speedway. Mack Smith, another Board of Fair Commissioners member, said the speedway contributed only about 10-15% of the revenue used to run the fairgrounds. Both Wilson and Smith pointed out that the fairgrounds received substantial revenue from the Tennessee State Fair, the monthly flea market operation, the rental of buildings throughout the year, and rent received from the Fair Park operations. Some of the councilmen voiced concerns about the efficiency of running both venues. There was an unspoken inference that Mr. Donoho, a former Assistant Police Chief for Nashville, was convicted in 1966, of filing false income tax returns. Donoho was not realistically considered for the opportunity to promote the Municipal Auditorium.

In a meeting of the Metro Fair Board, efforts to force Donoho to make an estimated $30,000 repair to the facility's leaking roof were handed over to the Metro Legal Department, which tried to negotiate with Donoho's attorney. Fairgrounds Manager Ted Vaughan said a legal opinion from Metro Attorney William F. Howard indicated Donoho's lease with the Fair Board made him responsible for roof maintenance. "I've been here 21 years, and I've never spent a penny on the roof," Donoho told the board. "The Fair Board has maintained it [the roof] and has had the insurance on it," Vaughan stated. As a matter of fact, the insurance company that the Fair Board had its policy with ruled that the leak was caused by winter damage. The insurance company claimed the damage was due to freezing, which was not one of the named liabilities and was not covered in the policy. Therefore, Donoho's lease made him responsible for the repairs. Vaughan said minor repairs had been done in the past by fairground employees. Bids from two firms indicated the cost would be between $20,000 and $50,000 to repair it. The Fair Board voiced that it was time Donoho began paying for repairs.

****

Rain, Rain, Go Away!
You're interfering with my schedule,
All this rain, floods, and delays,
For my business is detrimental.

****

Bill Donoho was often frustrated with the weather. The heavy rains forced the postponement of the Winston 500 at Talladega. This brought about some conflict with Music City 420 scheduled for the Fairgrounds Speedway. The Music City 420 had to be postponed until late spring. "Why does my race get the rain date because of the previous rainout of Winston 500? It makes no sense," Mr. Donoho lamented. Donoho was also angered by the rain that fell through the roof of the speedway, which the Fair Board now says (21 years later) was his responsibility to repair. The board tried to force Donoho to make an estimated $30,000 in repairs on the roof. Fairgrounds Manager Ted Vaughan repeated the legal opinion from Metro Attorney William F. Howard had stated that Donoho's lease made him responsible for roof maintenance.

37. Guitar Pool Dispute

"If you like a person, you say 'let's go into business together.' Man is a social animal after all, but such partnerships are fraught with danger."

– Brian Tracy

Webb Pierce and Fairgrounds Speedway promoter Bill Donoho announced plans in 1977, to build a replica on Music Row of the guitar-shaped pool at Pierce's home in Oak Hill. Tourists had been openly invited to Pierce's home to view the pool and other music memorabilia.

However, in November 1978, Webb Pierce and Bill Donoho had their partnership dispute over the Music Row Pool end in a court standoff. The spat between entertainer Webb Pierce and the Bill Donoho family over managing the controversial Music Row swimming pool ended in a draw. Jim Donoho, President of the "non-profit corporation," his father, and Pierce formed the non-profit to build the swimming pool. They asked Chancery Court on October 24, 1978, to oust Pierce from the Board of Directors. The suit also asked the court to order Pierce to return his 19 gold records and silver-dollar-studded 1962 Pontiac to the pool on Music Square East. Pierce's attorney, Howard Butler, filed a motion just before the hearing asking Chancellor C. Allen High to dismiss the suit because Jim Donoho "had no authority to bring this suit without prior approval of the Board of Directors." But the Donohos' attorney, Stan

Allen, replied, "the Board of Directors cannot agree that it's daylight outside." Chancellor High surprised both sides in the lawsuit, citing a law giving him authority to dissolve a non-profit corporation if the directors couldn't agree on how it should be managed. The presiding Judge gave Stan Allen seven days to file a reply to Butler's motion, then would dismiss the lawsuit. "If the suit is not in the correct posture, we'll get it in the correct posture." Stan Allen said after the hearing. "We're not pursuing dissolution, but if that's the only legal cure available to us, we may have to swallow it," After the hearing, Attorney Butler declared that the pool would open the following summer. Butler's statement implied a resolution was close. Pierce, and both Jr. and Sr. Donohos, attended the hearing but deferred any questions to their attorneys.

However, after the Oak Hill community filed complaints to officials, the courts ordered Pierce to discontinue tours to his home. Pierce and the elder Donoho formed D.D. & P. Inc., officially a non-profit corporation, so that they could get zoning approval for the construction of the pool. The elder Donoho and his wife Mildred, Pierce, and Max T. Powell, a longtime associate of Pierce, were on the non-profit's Board of Directors. That corporation then contracted with Donoho/Pierce Promotions, a partnership owned by Pierce and the elder Donoho, to operate the pool, with the younger Donoho as general manager. The pool opened and charged $2 for admission and $10 for membership in the Webb Pierce Hall of Fame for Country Music Fans. Purchasers of memberships were entitled to have their names engraved on the brass border around the pool.

Jim Donoho filed the lawsuit alleging that Pierce "had intentionally created havoc, chaos, and confusion" in the operation of the pool. The lawsuit also alleged that Pierce put his former employees on the corporation's payroll and wrote checks on the corporation without the approval of the Board of Directors. A brief was filed alleging that Jim Donoho only filed the suit "in retaliation for his dismissal as manager and president of the corporation and for failure to be present at the pool during working hours, managing the business in an incompetent manner," said Attorney Butler.

38. The Dispute Continues

The Bill Donoho Soap Opera Continues

"We need not worry so much about what man descends from; it is what he descends to that shames the human race."

– Mark Twain

Mr. Webb Pierce and Mr. Bill Donoho entertained Nashville with a real-life soap opera over the guitar-shaped pool. It all began when they decided to become partners in Webb Pierce's Hall of Fame for Country Music Fans. That was after Mr. Donoho sold the Nashville Speedways and all the furor over Mr. Pierce signing autographs and selling records to long lines of tourists around his backyard guitar-shaped swimming pool on Curtiswood Lane in Oak Hill.

The fighting began when Pierce removed his silver-dollar-studded 1962 Pontiac and 19 Gold Records from the Hall of Fame and changed its locks. Both Donohos were deliberately locked out. Later, Donoho retaliated by dumping catfish into the guitar-shaped pool inside the Hall of Fame. The pool was a replica of the swimming pool behind Pierce's home. Donoho said he planned to turn the Hall of Fame into "something everyone can enjoy."

The two men had to face each other once more in court due to a lawsuit filed by Third National Bank for unpaid bills. The suit also alleged that Pierce withdrew $7,759 from a joint account without Donoho's signature, as required.

This partnership was mixing water and acid the wrong way—explosive. The former friends began calling each other names in public.

In court, the Music Row Pool and Hall of Fame owners continued with name-calling and references to Donoho's 1968 conviction on federal income tax evasion charges. Pierce claimed he didn't know Donoho was an ex-convict until he went into business with him. Donoho fired back, stating that he didn't know Pierce was an alcoholic until he went into business with him. The two continued to verbally spar against one another, creating entertainment gossip fodder for the entire community.

39. A Plunderer

What happened to the law violators who testified in William "Bill" Donoho's legal battles regarding tax evasion in the 1950s and 1960s? To quote radio personality Paul Harvey, "now you know the rest of the story."

William H. "Bill" Frazier (not related to my Great-Uncle Bill Donoho, of whom this book is written) was buried on August 26, 1979, in Cheatam County, Tennessee. He was 70 years old and had been terminally ill for several years. William H. "Bill" Frazier was known as a gambler for over 40 years in some of Nashville's under-belly, illegal activities. Events of his life contributed to some of the most bizarre and colorful episodic periods. Ironically, Frazier was a well-known police character. He was born and raised in Ashland City but moved to Davidson County as a young man. He worked many jobs during his twenties, sometimes in law clerks' offices, at service stations, and at the Pie Wagon on Gallatin Road. In his later years, he openly bragged about his illegal pursuits, chiefly gambling and working the numbers racket. However, as the convicted slayer of a Greek cleaning parlor proprietor, Frazier was most widely known. The murder victim, George Johnson, was slain in 1939 during what police termed a war between the city's Greek hatters. His beaten body was found on Old River Road across the Cumberland River from Ashland City. The slaying initiated one of the most bizarre murder mysteries in Nashville's criminal history.

Johnson was a wealthy member of the city's Greek community and operator of the Palace Hatters, a cleaning establishment on Fourth Avenue, North, downtown Nashville. Three of his competitors were accused of hiring Frazier, who was then 30 and already known as an ex-convict, to kidnap Johnson and murder him. After a lengthy and widely publicized trial of kidnapping Johnson from near his home on Kenner Avenue, shooting him in the head, and dumping his body, Frazier was convicted and sentenced to life in prison. Incarceration was familiar territory for Frazier. He had previously served two years for conspiracy to violate the Federal Dyer Act, a stolen car statute. Among his convictions, he had been convicted of carrying a pistol.

His familiarity with Correctional Institutions led him later to say he had "free run of the whole inside of the prison" here in Nashville. He was incarcerated from 1939 to 1952. While behind bars at the Tennessee State Penitentiary, Frazier made money gambling with his fellow inmates. He had been a gambler before the murder conviction. He also hauled bootleg whiskey during the Depression years, going as far away as Illinois to get the illegal booze to sell in bootlegging joints that he operated in Nashville.

In 1952, former Mayor Tom Cummings represented Frazier to get parole. One prison official described Frazier as "an indispensable man" in the prison's metal plant where he worked. "I believe him to be rehabilitated to the extent that he would be an asset to society," the official told the parole board. That effort to gain parole failed, but later in the year, his sentence was commuted by then-Governor Gordon Browning, and he was freed.

Back on the streets, Frazier continued his life of crime. By most accounts, he became the "Kingpin" of Nashville's number racket operations. Frazier, a cigar-smoking man who was ruggedly handsome when young, was always rather proud of his underworld operations and the reputation he insisted he had as "being the first man on the street with the money" to pay off winners in the numbers business.

He operated virtually unmolested for years because of a known friendly relationship with some police officers. In the 1960s, it was made public how Frazier allegedly cultivated his social relations with the police. Then, under pressure from Internal Revenue Service agents, he turned over to federal officials a list of city police officers he claimed he had paid over a period of six years for the privilege of being allowed to conduct his illegal activities. Later, in 1966, he testified in federal court that former Assistant Police Chief "Wild Bill" Donoho was among "140 or 150" police officers he paid off. At the time of his testimony, he was free on appeal from a five-year sentence in which he had received prison for income tax evasion. The irony shows a pattern of opportunities the two "Wild Bills'" encountered with one another from time to time. He dove deep into the seriousness of organized crime on the streets of Nashville. William "Bill" Frazier was a man of considerable influence in prison and out as a free man, plundering the people of Nashville.

40. End of the Empire

Hard Times Fall on Young William James (Jim) Donoho Jr.

"Boogity, Boogity, Boogity! Let's Go Racin' Boys!"
— Darrell Waltrip

In 1983, Nashville race promoter Jim Donoho had to file bankruptcy, citing over $10 million in personal debts and only $900 in assets. Jim Donoho listed debts that included $10 million in damages from an automobile crash lawsuit filed by Mr. and Mrs. Joseph Patanzo of Phoenix, Arizona. He also listed a $2,000 1975 debt for his automobile, $13,000 to Hank Elmendorf of Phoenix for a 1981 video race film, $2,000 to Hildebrand & Associates for 1982 divorce fees, $6,000 to Murfreesboro Bank & Trust Company for a 1975 loan, and $800 to Levy's for clothing charges in 1974. Donoho from Hermitage, Tennessee, claimed assets of $400 in clothes and jewelry, $400 for insurance policies, and $100 for copyright. As his father had done, he fell from grace only to rise only a few years later.

Love found Jim Donoho again in a third marriage, this time to Linda. Like his father, he rose to live another day with fresh ideas, new business partners, and a never-give-up ideology. Along with his unique sense of manly purpose, his new bride, and his opportunity for a fresh start or a do-over, if you will, Jim found new purpose.

In 1988, Bill Donoho and his son Jim Donoho offered Nashvillians a one-hour oil change, lube, filter, and inspection service for truck drivers and fleets. Bill Donoho and Jim were inspired by the success of Jiffy Lube and other companies that provide fluid and filter services for cars and small trucks, so they joined with truck maintenance veteran James Blackwood, owner of Blackwood Truck Repair, for the project. Jim Donoho felt strongly that their business was one of the first in the country, and original plans were in place to franchise the business. Their first facility was a three-bay center in one of the city's heaviest traffic districts at Elm Hill Pike and Fessler's Lane. "We look for 90% of our business to be local," Donoho said. The new enterprise tried establishing stable relationships with area companies operating small, medium, and large truck fleets. It was similar to the Jiffy Lube concept, but the pits were 65 feet long and could hold a tractor-trailer rig and provide services in one hour. Services included lubrication, air, and oil filter changes, brake inspection and adjustment, and a preventive maintenance and safety inspection covering the items inspected by the U.S. Department of Transportation. Jim Donoho clarified that the company did not do any maintenance, but promised unbiased evaluations of any maintenance that might be needed. The services were limited to diesel trucks of one ton and larger. The idea was to reduce truckers' downtime and give truckers alternatives to waiting for hours at one of the full-service truck shops for work that could be completed in one hour. Blackwood continued his repair business, which operated right off Cleveland Avenue, and received several referrals from Jim's new adventure business.

At the young age of 53, William James (Jim) Donoho Jr. passed quietly from complications of cancer in 2002. His father, Bill Donoho preceded him in death in 1993.

Conclusion

At this book's beginning, I asked, "What motivates a man of meager beginnings?" The answer to that question was answered throughout the chapters of this book. Bill Donoho was a master at networking and a legend while alive, with a reputation that stretched across this country. He developed relationships all over the country that helped create the man he was, as well as the man he became. He left an indelible legacy for Nashvillians, Tennesseans, NASCAR, the sport of stockcar racing, and the sobering real-life drama in which his life's breath, from birth to death, decreed his whole being always to move forward.

Bill Donoho passed away on March 1, 1993. He was 77 years old. The extraordinary life of William James Donoho Sr. *(also known as 'Wild Bill in many corners and smokey rooms)* was much to be admired. He was born struggling to survive and lived a life of wealth, power, authority, and memorable escapades as a Davidson County Police Officer, a World War II Veteran, a leader of American Legion Post #5, an avid sportsman with rifle and gun skills that could compare to no other, a convict who spent time out of state in Federal Prison, principal owner and investor of the Nashville Fairgrounds Speedway which brought a great deal of tourism and publicity to Nashville and the state of Tennessee, as well as the racing world nationally and internationally. He was a risk taker and clearly shared his innovative brilliance with his son Jim, who tried to inspire an imprint on the world just as his father had. He left a broad footprint on the state of Tennessee and the world. The ebbs and flow of "Wild Bill" Donoho's etching on this state and its people cannot be denied.

I'm proud of my heritage. My ancestors were just people with a conviction to live. To live by any means possible. I think we are all survivors of our past, and those who live through it, learn from it, and push on toward the finish line, will always get the checkered flag.

Bibliography

February 14, 1930 (page 11 of 22). (1930, Feb 14). *Nashville Tennessean (1923-1972)*

October 29, 1941 (page 1 of 16). (1941, Oct 29). *Nashville Tennessean (1923-1972)*

September 12, 1942 (page 1 of 12). (1942, Sep 12). *Nashville Tennessean (1923-1972)*

September 12, 1942 (page 2 of 12). (1942, Sep 12). *Nashville Tennessean (1923-1972)*

October 11, 1942 (page 19 of 98). (1942, Oct 11). *Nashville Tennessean (1923-1972)*

January 2, 1945 (page 22 of 22). (1945, Jan 02). *Nashville Tennessean (1923-1972)*

November 5, 1945 (page 4 of 16). (1945, Nov 05). *Nashville Tennessean (1923-1972)*

June 21, 1946 (page 1 of 44). (1946, Jun 21). *Nashville Tennessean (1923-1972)*

June 21, 1946 (page 4 of 44). (1946, Jun 21). *Nashville Tennessean (1923-1972)*

July 28, 1946 (page 54 of 116). (1946, Jul 28). *Nashville Tennessean (1923-1972)*

August 18, 1946 (page 51 of 92). (1946, Aug 18). *Nashville Tennessean (1923-1972)*

September 19, 1947 (page 33 of 44). (1947, Sep 19). *Nashville Tennessean (1923-1972)*

October 11, 1947 (page 1 of 8). (1947, Oct 11). *Nashville Tennessean (1923-1972)*

October 11, 1947 (page 2 of 8). (1947, Oct 11). *Nashville Tennessean (1923-1972)*

October 22, 1947 (page 16 of 26). (1947, Oct 22). *Nashville Tennessean (1923-1972)*

October 28, 1947 (page 13 of 24). (1947, Oct 28). *Nashville Tennessean (1923-1972)*

November 1, 1947 (page 3 of 8). (1947, Nov 01). *Nashville Tennessean (1923-1972)*

November 6, 1947 (page 12 of 34). (1947, Nov 06). *Nashville Tennessean (1923-1972)*

November 23, 1947 (page 69 of 106). (1947, Nov 23). *Nashville Tennessean (1923-1972)*

March 30, 1948 (page 12 of 22). (1948, Mar 30). *Nashville Tennessean (1923-1972)*

April 7, 1948 (page 15 of 26). (1948, Apr 07). *Nashville Tennessean (1923-1972)*

May 29, 1948 (page 5 of 12). (1948, May 29). *Nashville Tennessean (1923-1972)*

August 11, 1948 (page 13 of 24). (1948, Aug 11). *Nashville Tennessean (1923-1972)*

July 10, 1949 (page 1 of 103). (1949, Jul 10). *Nashville Tennessean (1923-1972)*

July 10, 1949 (page 4 of 103). (1949, Jul 10). *Nashville Tennessean (1923-1972)*

July 13, 1949 (page 16 of 28). (1949, Jul 13). *Nashville Tennessean (1923-1972)*

July 23, 1949 (page 10 of 14). (1949, Jul 23). *Nashville Tennessean (1923-1972)*

September 9, 1949 (page 17 of 59). (1949, Sep 09). *Nashville Tennessean (1923-1972)*

June 27, 1950 (page 8 of 28). (1950, Jun 27). *Nashville Tennessean (1923-1972)*

July 9, 1950 (page 10 of 102). (1950, Jul 09). *Nashville Tennessean (1923-1972)*

July 10, 1950 (page 15 of 19). (1950, Jul 10). *Nashville Tennessean (1923-1972)*

August 26, 1951 (page 13 of 121). (1951, Aug 26). *Nashville Tennessean (1923-1972)*

January 4, 1952 (page 1 of 41). (1952, Jan 04). *Nashville Tennessean (1923-1972)*

June 23, 1952 (page 16 of 20). (1952, Jun 23). *Nashville Tennessean (1923-1972)*

July 17, 1952 (page 3 of 35). (1952, Jul 17). *Nashville Tennessean (1923-1972)*

July 28, 1952 (page 5 of 18). (1952, Jul 28). *Nashville Tennessean (1923-1972)*

August 2, 1952 (page 1 of 16). (1952, Aug 02). *Nashville Tennessean (1923-1972)*

August 2, 1952 (page 2 of 16). (1952, Aug 02). *Nashville Tennessean (1923-1972)*

November 1, 1952 (page 10 of 21). (1952, Nov 01). *Nashville Tennessean (1923-1972)*

January 16, 1953 (page 19 of 50). (1953, Jan 16). *Nashville Tennessean (1923-1972)*

January 19, 1953 (page 3 of 18). (1953, Jan 19). *Nashville Tennessean (1923-1972)*

March 8, 1953 (page 28 of 122). (1953, Mar 08). *Nashville Tennessean (1923-1972)*

April 28, 1953 (page 1 of 30). (1953, Apr 28). *Nashville Tennessean (1923-1972)*

April 28, 1953 (page 4 of 30). (1953, Apr 28). *Nashville Tennessean (1923-1972)*

August 11, 1953 (page 1 of26). (1953, Aug 11). *Nashville Tennessean (1923-1972)*

November 10, 1953 (page 24 of 29). (1953, Nov 10). *Nashville Tennessean (1923-1972)*

August 13, 1954 (page 13 of 55). (1954, Aug 13). *Nashville Tennessean (1923-1972)*

September 13, 1954 (page 1 of 24). (1954, Sep 13). *Nashville Tennessean (1923-1972)*

September 13, 1954 (page 4 of 24). (1954, Sep 13). *Nashville Tennessean (1923-1972)*

May 13, 1955 (page 14 of 67). (1955, May 13). *Nashville Tennessean (1923-1972)*

September 5, 1955 (page 13 of 22). (1955, Sep 05). *Nashville Tennessean (1923-1972)*

April 20, 1956 (page 21 of 64). (1956, Apr 20). *Nashville Tennessean (1923-1972)*

May 3, 1956 (page 35 of 40). (1956, May 03). *Nashville Tennessean (1923-1972)*

August 1, 1956 (page 25 of 30). (1956, Aug 01). *Nashville Tennessean (1923-1972)*

November 3, 1956 (page 14 of 18). (1956, Nov 03). *Nashville Tennessean (1923-1972)*

November 7, 1956 (page 18 of 36). (1956, Nov 07). *Nashville Tennessean (1923-1972)*

March 23, 1957 (page 12 of 16). (1957, Mar 23). *Nashville Tennessean (1923-1972)*

May 1, 1957 (page 28 of 32). (1957, May 01). *Nashville Tennessean (1923-1972)*

August 29, 1957 (page 23 of 39). (1957, Aug 29). *Nashville Tennessean (1923-1972)*

November 24, 1957 (page 17 of 132). (1957, Nov 24). *Nashville Tennessean (1923-1972)*

April 14, 1958 (page 2 of 22). (1958, Apr 14). *Nashville Tennessean (1923-1972)*

April 26, 1958 (page 1 of 21). (1958, Apr 26). *Nashville Tennessean (1923-1972)*

April 26, 1958 (page 2 of 21). (1958, Apr 26). *Nashville Tennessean (1923-1972)*

November 11, 1958 (page 26 of 26). (1958, Nov 11). *Nashville Tennessean (1923-1972)*

December 18, 1959 (page 18 of 56). (1959, Dec 18). *Nashville Tennessean (1923-1972)*

April 17, 1960 (page 18 of 110). (1960, Apr 17). *Nashville Tennessean (1923-1972)*

June 23, 1960 (page 1 of 50). (1960, Jun 23). *Nashville Tennessean (1923-1972)*

June 23, 1960 (page 10 of 50). (1960, Jun 23). *Nashville Tennessean (1923-1972)*

October 1, 1960 (page 3 of 20). (1960, Oct 01). *Nashville Tennessean (1923-1972)*

January 2, 1961 (page 12 of 37). (1961, Jan 02). *Nashville Tennessean (1923-1972)*

January 18, 1961 (page 4 of 24). (1961, Jan 18). *Nashville Tennessean (1923-1972)*

July 18, 1961 (page 3 of 24). (1961, Jul 18). *Nashville Tennessean (1923-1972)*

July 22, 1961 (page 7 of 22). (1961, Jul 22). *Nashville Tennessean (1923-1972)*

January 24, 1962 (page 15 of 24). (1962, Jan 24). *Nashville Tennessean (1923-1972)*

January 28, 1962 (page 43 of 92). (1962, Jan 28). *Nashville Tennessean (1923-1972)*

March 10, 1962 (page 8 of 20). (1962, Mar 10). *Nashville Tennessean (1923-1972)*

January 5, 1963 (page 3 of 20). (1963, Jan 05). *Nashville Tennessean (1923-1972)*

January 13, 1963 (page 1 of 126). (1963, Jan 13). *Nashville Tennessean (1923-1972)*

January 13, 1963 (page 6 of 126). (1963, Jan 13).
Nashville Tennessean (1923-1972)

February 1, 1963 (page 10 of 42). (1963, Feb 01).
Nashville Tennessean (1923-1972)

March 9, 1963 (page 9 of 22). (1963, Mar 09).
Nashville Tennessean (1923-1972)

March 12, 1963 (page 28 of 28). (1963, Mar 12).
Nashville Tennessean (1923-1972)

March 19, 1963 (page 14 of 26). (1963, Mar 19).
Nashville Tennessean (1923-1972)

March 25, 1963 (page 1 of 24). (1963, Mar 25).
Nashville Tennessean (1923-1972)

March 25, 1963 (page 4 of 24). (1963, Mar 25).
Nashville Tennessean (1923-1972)

March 31, 1963 (page 19 of 133). (1963, Mar 31).
Nashville Tennessean (1923-1972)

May 30, 1963 (page 1 of 67). (1963, May 30).
Nashville Tennessean (1923-1972)

May 30, 1963 (page 10 of 67). (1963, May 30).
Nashville Tennessean (1923-1972)

October 5, 1963 (page 16 of 24). (1963, Oct 05).
Nashville Tennessean (1923-1972)

March 18, 1964 (page 2 of 30). (1964, Mar 18).
Nashville Tennessean (1923-1972)

March 19, 1964 (page 1 of 68). (1964, Mar 19).
Nashville Tennessean (1923-1972)

March 19, 1964 (page 14 of 68). (1964, Mar 19).
Nashville Tennessean (1923-1972)

June 18, 1964 (page 1 of 71). (1964, Jun 18).
Nashville Tennessean (1923-1972)

June 18, 1964 (page 11 of 71). (1964, Jun 18).
Nashville Tennessean (1923-1972)

March 18, 1964 (page 2 of 30). (1964, Mar 18). *Nashville Tennessean (1923-1972)*

June 20, 1964 (page 12 of 26). (1964, Jun 20). *Nashville Tennessean (1923-1972)*

July 28, 1964 (page 4 of 24). (1964, Jul 28). *Nashville Tennessean (1923-1972)*

August 13, 1964 (page 12 of 103). (1964, Aug 13). *Nashville Tennessean (1923-1972)*

August 26, 1964 (page 19 of 32). (1964, Aug 26). *Nashville Tennessean (1923-1972)*

September 11, 1964 (page 1 of 53). (1964, Sep 11). *Nashville Tennessean (1923-1972)*

September 11, 1964 (page 7 of 53). (1964, Sep 11). *Nashville Tennessean (1923-1972)*

October 1, 1964 (page 16 of 77). (1964, Oct 01). *Nashville Tennessean (1923-1972)*

October 4, 1964 (page 32 of 145). (1964, Oct 04). *Nashville Tennessean (1923-1972)*

October 6, 1964 (page 1 of 28). (1964, Oct 06). *Nashville Tennessean (1923-1972)*

October 6, 1964 (page 4 of 28). (1964, Oct 06). *Nashville Tennessean (1923-1972)*

October 7, 1964 (page 4 of 28). (1964, Oct 07). *Nashville Tennessean (1923-1972)*

October 8, 1964 (page 1 of 59). (1964, Oct 08). *Nashville Tennessean (1923-1972)*

October 8, 1964 (page 6 of 59). (1964, Oct 08). *Nashville Tennessean (1923-1972)*

December 20, 1964 (page 59 of 110). (1964, Dec 20). *Nashville Tennessean (1923-1972)*

March 25, 1965 (page 2 of 74). (1965, Mar 25). *Nashville Tennessean (1923-1972)*

March 26, 1965 (page 20 of 50). (1965, Mar 26). *Nashville Tennessean (1923-1972)*

May 7, 1965 (page 26 of 54). (1965, May 07). *Nashville Tennessean (1923-1972)*

May 11, 1965 (page 22 of 28). (1965, May 11). *Nashville Tennessean (1923-1972)*

May 19, 1965 (page 6 of 33). (1965, May 19). *Nashville Tennessean (1923-1972)*

July 13, 1965 (page 7 of 24). (1965, Jul 13). *Nashville Tennessean (1923-1972)*

July 15, 1965 (page 53 of 60). (1965, Jul 15). *Nashville Tennessean (1923-1972)*

October 8, 1965 (page 3 of 64). (1965, Oct 08). *Nashville Tennessean (1923-1972)*

October 29, 1965 (page 9 of 48). (1965, Oct 29). *Nashville Tennessean (1923-1972)*

October 31, 1965 (page 19 of 145). (1965, Oct 31). *Nashville Tennessean (1923-1972)*

October 31, 1965 (page 19 of 145). (1965, Oct 31). *Nashville Tennessean (1923-1972)*

December 2, 1965 (page 56 of 97). (1965, Dec 02). *Nashville Tennessean (1923-1972)*

December 5, 1965 (page 24 of 236). (1965, Dec 05). *Nashville Tennessean (1923-1972)*

December 19, 1965 (page 12 of 143). (1965, Dec 19). *Nashville Tennessean (1923-1972)*

December 23, 1965 (page 22 of 28). (1965, Dec 23). *Nashville Tennessean (1923-1972)*

May 17, 1966 (page 1 of 34). (1966, May 17). *Nashville Tennessean (1923-1972)*

May 17, 1966 (page 2 of 34). (1966, May 17). *Nashville Tennessean (1923-1972)*

July 24, 1966 (page 143 of 263). (1966, Jul 24). *Nashville Tennessean (1923-1972)*

October 8, 1966 (page 1 of 28). (1966, Oct 08). *Nashville Tennessean (1923-1972)*

October 8, 1966 (page 2 of 28). (1966, Oct 08). *Nashville Tennessean (1923-1972)*

October 23, 1966 (page 1 of 174). (1966, Oct 23). *Nashville Tennessean (1923-1972)*

October 23, 1966 (page 16 of 174). (1966, Oct 23). *Nashville Tennessean (1923-1972)*

October 24, 1966 (page 1 of 30). (1966, Oct 24). *Nashville Tennessean (1923-1972)*

October 24, 1966 (page 2 of 30). (1966, Oct 24). *Nashville Tennessean (1923-1972)*

October 25, 1966 (page 2 of 28). (1966, Oct 25). *Nashville Tennessean (1923-1972)*

October 26, 1966 (page 1 of 41). (1966, Oct 26). *Nashville Tennessean (1923-1972)*

October 26, 1966 (page 5 of 41). (1966, Oct 26). *Nashville Tennessean (1923-1972)*

October 27, 1966 (page 2 of 72). (1966, Oct 27). *Nashville Tennessean (1923-1972)*

October 28, 1966 (page 13 of 50). (1966, Oct 28). *Nashville Tennessean (1923-1972)*

October 29, 1966 (page 1 of 30). (1966, Oct 29). *Nashville Tennessean (1923-1972)*

October 29, 1966 (page 2 of 30). (1966, Oct 29). *Nashville Tennessean (1923-1972)*

October 30, 1966 (page 5 of 136). (1966, Oct 30). *Nashville Tennessean (1923-1972)*

October 31, 1966 (page 1 of 32). (1966, Oct 31). *Nashville Tennessean (1923-1972)*

October 29, 1966 (page 1 of 30). (1966, Oct 31).*Nashville Tennessean (1923-1972)*

October 31, 1966 (page 5 of 32). (1966, Oct 31). *Nashville Tennessean (1923-1972)*

November 1, 1966 (page 1 of 28). (1966, Nov 01). *Nashville Tennessean (1923-1972)*

November 1, 1966 (page 4 of 28). (1966, Nov 01). *Nashville Tennessean (1923-1972)*

November 2, 1966 (page 1 of 41). (1966, Nov 02). *Nashville Tennessean (1923-1972)*

November 2, 1966 (page 8 of 41). (1966, Nov 02). *Nashville Tennessean (1923-1972)*

November 3, 1966 (page 2 of 92). (1966, Nov 03). *Nashville Tennessean (1923-1972)*

November 4, 1966 (page 1 of 50). (1966, Nov 04). *Nashville Tennessean (1923-1972)*

November 4, 1966 (page 8 of 50). (1966, Nov 04). *Nashville Tennessean (1923-1972)*

November 5, 1966 (page 4 of 35). (1966, Nov 05). *Nashville Tennessean (1923-1972)*

November 8, 1966 (page 6 of 28). (1966, Nov 08). *Nashville Tennessean (1923-1972)*

November 19, 1966 (page 28 of 28). (1966, Nov 19). *Nashville Tennessean (1923-1972)*

November 20, 1966 (page 23 of 161). (1966, Nov 20). *Nashville Tennessean (1923-1972)*

November 22, 1966 (page 1 of 37). (1966, Nov 22). *Nashville Tennessean (1923-1972)*

November 22, 1966 (page 2 of 37). (1966, Nov 22). *Nashville Tennessean (1923-1972)*

December 2, 1966 (page 22 of 62). (1966, Dec 02). *Nashville Tennessean (1923-1972)*

March 15, 1967 (page 32 of 45). (1967, Mar 15). *Nashville Tennessean (1923-1972)*

March 31, 1967 (page 5 of 48). (1967, Mar 31). *Nashville Tennessean (1923-1972)*

April 29, 1967 (page 28 of 28). (1967, Apr 29). *Nashville Tennessean (1923-1972)*

July 23, 1967 (page 127 of 139). (1967, Jul 23). *Nashville Tennessean (1923-1972)*

November 5, 1967 (page 22 of 199). (1967, Nov 05). *Nashville Tennessean (1923-1972*

November 30, 1967 (page 64 of 73). (1967, Nov 30). *Nashville Tennessean (1923-1972)*

January 27, 1968 (page 9 of 24). (1968, Jan 27). *Nashville Tennessean (1923-1972)*

April 10, 1968 (page 7 of 38). (1968, Apr 10). *Nashville Tennessean (1923-1972)*

April 17, 1968 (page 13 of 45). (1968, Apr 17). *Nashville Tennessean (1923-1972)*

April 24, 1968 (page 6 of 53). (1968, Apr 24). *Nashville Tennessean (1923-1972)*

June 30, 1968 (page 79 of 84). (1968, Jun 30). *Nashville Tennessean (1923-1972)*

December 28, 1968 (page 19 of 26). (1968, Dec 28). *Nashville Tennessean (1923-1972)*

January 31, 1969 (page 28 of 44). (1969, Jan 31). *Nashville Tennessean (1923-1972)*

June 5, 1969 (page 3 of 95). (1969, Jun 05). *Nashville Tennessean (1923-1972)*

June 26, 1969 (page 63 of 85). (1969, Jun 26). *Nashville Tennessean (1923-1972)*

July 20, 1969 (page 81 of 148). (1969, Jul 20). *Nashville Tennessean (1923-1972)*

July 20, 1969 (page 83 of 148). (1969, Jul 20). *Nashville Tennessean (1923-1972)*

July 20, 1969 (page 94 of 148). (1969, Jul 20). *Nashville Tennessean (1923-1972)*

December 21, 1969 (page 1 of 150). (1969, Dec 21). *Nashville Tennessean (1923-1972)*

December 24, 1969 (page 2 of 26). (1969, Dec 24). *Nashville Tennessean (1923-1972)*

December 28, 1969 (page 1 of 149). (1969, Dec 28). *Nashville Tennessean (1923-1972)*

December 28, 1969 (page 6 of 149). (1969, Dec 28). *Nashville Tennessean (1923-1972)*

January 4, 1970 (page 6 of 143). (1970, Jan 04). *Nashville Tennessean (1923-1972)*

January 9, 1970 (page 2 of 36). (1970, Jan 09). *Nashville Tennessean (1923-1972)*

January 22, 1970 (page 2 of 60). (1970, Jan 22). *Nashville Tennessean (1923-1972)*

July 6, 1970 (page 5 of 31). (1970, Jul 06). *Nashville Tennessean (1923-1972*

August 19, 1970 (page 32 of 53). (1970, Aug 19). *Nashville Tennessean (1923-1972)*

May 26, 1971 (page 35 of 66). (1971, May 26). *Nashville Tennessean (1923-1972)*

July 11, 1971 (page 89 of 154). (1971, Jul 11). *Nashville Tennessean (1923-1972)*

July 11, 1971 (page 90 of 154). (1971, Jul 11). *Nashville Tennessean (1923-1972)*

July 18, 1971 (page 96 of 136). (1971, Jul 18). *Nashville Tennessean (1923-1972)*

August 4, 1971 (page 30 of 65). (1971, Aug 04). *Nashville Tennessean (1923-1972)*

December 10, 1971 (page 35 of 69). (1971, Dec 10). *Nashville Tennessean (1923-1972)*

February 14, 1973 (page 34 of 44). (1973, Feb 14). *The Tennessean (1972-2002)*

May 3, 1973 (page 45 of 83). (1973, May 03). *The Tennessean (1972-2002)*

January 13, 1974 (page 81 of 268). (1974, Jan 13). *The Tennessean (1972-2002*

October 6, 1974 (page 24 of 186). (1974, Oct 06). *The Tennessean (1972-2002)*

January 16, 1976 (page 26 of 63). (1976, Jan 16). *The Tennessean (1972-2002)*

January 16, 1976 (page 61 of 63). (1976, Jan 16). *The Tennessean (1972-2002)*

July 26, 1976 (page 34 of 40). (1976, Jul 26). *The Tennessean (1972-2002)*

February 14, 1977 (page 1 of 41). (1977, Feb 14). *The Tennessean (1972-2002)*

April 21, 1978 (page 26 of 73). (1978, Apr 21). *The Tennessean (1972-2002)*

April 27, 1978 (page 24 of 84). (1978, Apr 27). *The Tennessean (1972-2002)*

May 11, 1978 (page 12 of 84). (1978, May 11). *The Tennessean (1972-2002)*

July 15, 1978 (page 1 of 34). (1978, Jul 15). *The Tennessean (1972-2002)*

July 19, 1978 (page 27 of 55). (1978, Jul 19). *The Tennessean (1972-2002)*

July 19, 1978 (page 30 of 55). (1978, Jul 19). *The Tennessean (1972-2002)*

November 8, 1978 (page 29 of 63). (1978, Nov 08). *The Tennessean (1972-2002)*

March 9, 1979 (page 1 of 54). (1979, Mar 09). *The Tennessean (1972-2002)*

March 9, 1979 (page 6 of 54). (1979, Mar 09). *The Tennessean (1972-2002)*

March 12, 1979 (page 6 of 48). (1979, Mar 12). *The Tennessean (1972-2002)*

August 25, 1979 (page 3 of 34). (1979, Aug 25). *The Tennessean (1972-2002)*

September 23, 1980 (page 20 of 44). (1980, Sep 23). *The Tennessean (1972-2002)*

October 13, 1983 (page 18 of 99). (1983, Oct 13). *The Tennessean (1972-2002)*

October 31, 1983 (page 10 of 32). (1983, Oct 31). *The Tennessean (1972-2002)*

November 2, 1984 (page 1 of 52). (1984, Nov 02). *The Tennessean (1972-2002)*

November 2, 1984 (page 12 of 52). (1984, Nov 02). *The Tennessean (1972-2002)*

December 26, 1984 (page 1 of 76). (1984, Dec 26). *The Tennessean (1972-2002)*

December 26, 1984 (page 10 of 76). (1984, Dec 26). *The Tennessean (1972-2002)*

March 7, 1985 (page 16 of 72). (1985, Mar 07). *The Tennessean (1972-2002)*

March 10, 1985 (page 10 of 216). (1985, Mar 10). *The Tennessean (1972-2002)*

May 10, 1985 (page 32 of 115). (1985, May 10). *The Tennessean (1972-2002)*

December 4, 1988 (page 61 of 624). (1988, Dec 04). *The Tennessean (1972-2002)*

July 19, 1992 (page 54 of 190). (1992, Jul 19). *The Tennessean (1972-2002)*

June 26, 2002 (page 17 of 81). (2002, Jun 26). *The Tennessean (1972-2002)*

Retrieved February 27, 2023, Wikipedia History of Wrestling

Retrieved February 27, 2023, Global Security, 1974 Inflation Crisis

About the Author

Shena Newberry Wilder is a graduate of David Lipscomb University (Nashville, Tennessee) and Tennessee Technological University (Cookville, Tennessee). She has experience in copy/content editing. She is a teacher and has taught in public and private schools most of her adult life. She enjoys reading, researching, and exploring history's miraculous romps through the strands of time. *Wild Bill Donoho: From Corrupt Cop to Raceway Mogul* is her second book.

Name Index

Made in the USA
Monee, IL
28 June 2023

37696374R00105